PARADOX
AND
PASSION
IN PSYCHOTHERAPY

WILEY SERIES
in
EXISTENTIAL PERSPECTIVES ON
PSYCHOTHERAPY AND COUNSELLING

Editor

Emmy van Deurzen

Existential Time-limited Therapy: The Wheel of Existence
Freddie Strasser and Alison Strasser

Case Studies in Existential Psychotherapy and Counselling
Editor: Simon du Plock

Paradox and Passion in Psychotherapy:
An Existential Approach to Therapy and Counselling
Emmy van Deurzen

Epidemiological
Research Methods

PARADOX
AND
PASSION
IN PSYCHOTHERAPY

AN EXISTENTIAL APPROACH
TO THERAPY
AND COUNSELLING

Emmy van Deurzen

JOHN WILEY & SONS

Chichester · New York · Weinheim · Brisbane · Singapore · Toronto

Published by John Wiley & Sons Ltd,
Baffins Lane, Chichester,
West Sussex PO19 1UD, England

National   01243 779777
International (+44) 1243 779777
e-mail (for orders and customer service enquiries):
cs-books@wiley.co.uk
Visit our Home Page on http://www.wiley.co.uk
or http://www.wiley.com

Other Wiley Editorial Offices

John Wiley & Sons, Inc., 605 Third Avenue,
New York, NY 10158-0012, USA

WILEY-VCH Verlag GmbH,
Pappelallee 3, D-69469 Weinheim, Germany

Jacaranda Wiley Ltd, 33 Park Road, Milton,
Queensland 4064, Australia

John Wiley & Sons (Asia) Pte Ltd, 2 Clementi Loop #02-01,
Jin Xing Distripark, Singapore 129809

John Wiley & Sons (Canada) Ltd, 22 Worcester Road,
Rexdale, Ontario M9W 1L1, Canada

Library of Congress Cataloging-in-Publication Data

Van Deurzen-Smith, Emmy.
    Paradox and passion in psychotherapy : an existential approach to
therapy and counselling / Emmy van Deurzen.
        p.   cm. — (Wiley series in existential psychotherapy and
counselling)
    Includes bibliographical references and index.
    ISBN 0-471-96191-4. — ISBN 0-471-97390-4 (pbk.)
    1. Existential psychotherapy.   I. Title.   II. Series.
RC489.E93V364   1998
616.89'14—dc21   97–49908
                                                                     CIP

British Library Cataloguing in Publication Data

A catalogue record for this book is available from the British Library

ISBN 0-471-96191-4 (cased)
ISBN 0-471-97390-4 (paper)

Typeset in 10/12 Palatino by Dorwyn Ltd, Rowlands Castle, Hants
Printed and bound in Great Britain by Bookcraft (Bath) Ltd, Midsomer Norton, Somerset
This book is printed on acid-free paper responsibly manufactured from sustainable forestry, in which at least two trees are planted for each one used for paper production.

To Digby
for bringing paradox and passion back to life

Infinite passion and the pain of finite hearts that yearn . . .

Robert Browning

CONTENTS

ABOUT THE AUTHOR

Emmy van Deurzen is a philosopher, counselling psychologist, and existential psychotherapist. She is the Director of the New School of Psychotherapy and Counselling at Schiller International University, London, where she is also Professor in Psychotherapy.

Previous to this she developed a number of degree courses in the field of counselling and psychotherapy, first for Antioch University International and then for Regent's College, London, where she was awarded a professorship for her outstanding contribution. Emmy founded the Society for Existential Analysis, which has provided a framework for the recognition and expansion of existential psychotherapy in the United Kingdom.

She has served as chair to the United Kingdom Council for Psychotherapy and is chair of the psychotherapy section of the British Psychological Society and vice-chair of the Universities Psychotherapy Association. She is External Relations Officer of the European Association for Psychotherapy and co-chairs its European Training Standards Committee, which has developed the European Certificate of Psychotherapy. She is much in demand as an international speaker on existential, social and political issues. She is the Series Editor for the Wiley Series in Existential Perspectives on Existential Psychotherapy and Counselling, and her previous publications include the books *Existential Counselling in Practice* and *Everyday Mysteries*.

Emmy has a private practice in Sheffield, where she is an Honorary Lecturer at the University and where she lives with her partner and the youngest of their four children.

SERIES PREFACE

Emmy van Deurzen

It is very telling that this series should be launched at a time when dramatic social and cultural changes accompany the turn of the millennium. As people contend with a sense of crisis and confusion they search for clarity and new ways of living. Increasingly they turn to the professions of psychotherapy and counselling to help them address crucial existential issues.

It is no longer sufficient to talk with clients and patients about their problems as if these were purely functions of intrapsychic mechanisms. In an increasingly complex world, people need to be able to see their own difficulties in relation to the overall contradictions and dilemmas that bedevil human living. They have to be able to make sense of themselves within their own context. Many human troubles are generated by living with technology, bureaucracy and social alienation. Other problems are as old as humanity itself and become more understandable when looked at from a philosophical angle.

The existential perspective on psychotherapy and counselling makes it possible to re-evaluate personal problems in the light of human wisdom. It pays attention to the philosophical, social, cultural and political dimensions as well as to the personal and the interpersonal. It encourages people to examine their lives and rediscover meaning. It makes room for paradox and the acceptance of the inevitable. It allows for questioning and re-evaluation.

Existential psychotherapy has been in existence for close to a century and the theories it is rooted in go back to the nineteenth century philosophies of freedom of Kierkegaard and Nietzsche and the twentieth century philosophies of Heidegger and Sartre, amongst others. Indirectly it draws on a much longer lineage, in that all of

Western and Eastern philosophy are relevant to such a reappraisal of everyday life.

The approach has not been well documented until quite recently, as many existential practitioners abhor formalization and technology and few have wanted to write about their work, let alone systematize it. This is a pity, for psychotherapists and counsellors need to inform each other of their findings about human life in order to progress in understanding the complex situations their clients are caught up in.

It is therefore delightful to me that the present series of books, with their focus on the application of the existential approach, will remedy this situation. Here are a number of practitioners documenting their own particular brand of existential work and showing it to be utterly relevant to their clients.

The present volume ranges widely from death to freedom and from the self to the concept of human communication. It discusses matters of relevance to every therapist's practice and raises more questions than it provides answers. In the final analysis, that is the main objective of the Series: to provoke and stimulate thought, not to add more prescriptions to psychotherapists or to dictate about a new professional method.

It is in reflecting on the human dilemma, and by looking at how existential psychotherapists deal concretely with their clients' specific predicaments, that our knowledge and understanding of our own lives will gradually improve.

PREFACE

Because of the dramatic ways in which my own life has been transformed over recent years, I have become more aware of the manner in which my psychotherapeutic work is responsive to the level of awareness that I can muster in my personal life. The quality of my work increases or decreases in accordance with the quality of my life. Throughout this book it will be clear that I want to encourage a more intense link between the way in which we live in the world and work with others towards greater understanding.

This does not mean that I advocate suffering or emotional upheavals. Interventions made during times of quietude can contribute calm, acceptance or even serenity. Interventions made in times of personal turmoil might contribute a higher level of personal resonance and direct insight. Neither is intrinsically better or worse, but I do believe that therapists can offer more to their clients if their work reflects an openness to the paradoxes of human living and if they are willing to live their own lives with full engagement and vitality. There are no short cuts to becoming a good psychotherapist or counsellor: skill alone might safeguard us from malpractice, but if we are to offer excellence we have to draw on the strengths that we can only acquire by living life intensely and bravely, with integrity and flexibility: with a complete readiness for what destiny holds in store for us.

We need to find the kind of equilibrium that is usually called wisdom and that is never quite mastered, but always within reach. I have come to believe that there is an optimum tension somewhere between complacency and catastrophe, which enables me to be secure enough to be steady and anxious enough to be alert, which serves both me and my clients best in managing life in all its contradictions. Somewhere between boredom and terror we can learn to be ourselves in harmony with the flow of life, rather than obstruct it or feel obstructed by it. This book represents my search for this optimum tension, and describes my own journey along the tortuous path, where moments of obstruction and stagnation co-exist with moments of new discoveries and flashes of insight that make it all worthwhile.

Some of the chapters in this book appeared as articles in a variety of publications at an earlier stage. They are the product of a decade of thinking and writing about psychotherapy and counselling and they speak for themselves. To publish these papers in this form is very satisfying to me, as it allows me to harvest the fruits of the past and store them safely for future use. That paradox and passion were present throughout the period when these words were written is abundantly obvious by the intense and perhaps sometimes controversial nature of what I say.

Some chapters highlight my concern with the establishment and safeguarding of the existential approach: something that I took very much to heart for many years. It resulted in me bringing together psychotherapists from a number of very different organizations and orientations in order to found the Society for Existential Analysis as a forum for philosophical debate and in order to secure a place for the approach in this country. The Society has now become a strong organization and the approach has been spread widely, partly because of the 18 years of hard work spent in building up a School of Psychotherapy and Counselling, first with Antioch University, then at Regent's College, where people could be trained in the existential approach. It is rather ironic that I have become dissociated from both the Society and the School when these have reached the maturity and mainstream credibility that I aimed for, and yet can now see the mortal dangers of. It is sad to have to let go of what one has created and it is hard to see others take these things into directions one did not want to go in oneself.

While I feel gratitude for having had the opportunity to bring these organizations into the world with the people who have cared for them with me, perhaps the greater existential lesson was to have to relinquish them. There is a tremendous excitement and exhilaration in having to start from scratch and no longer being able to take anything for granted, having to prove oneself worthy and able to survive. Founding the New School of Psychotherapy and Counselling and rediscovering the anxious pleasure of pioneering certainly put my own ability to live what I teach to the test.

Some other chapters refer directly to my experience as chair of the United Kingdom Council for Psychotherapy, which made me sensitive to the political and social dimensions of psychotherapy, which are so often neglected by professionals in this field. This political awareness has continued to increase through being external relations officer to the European Association for Psychotherapy, which has also inspired some of the writing in this book. It has become increasingly obvious to me that we need to take an international and trans-cultural view of human nature, working together to overcome the unnecessary conflicts and fears that stop us in our tracks.

The very personal nature of some of the chapters illustrates what I think is most precious in the existential approach: that it can be about life itself as it is actually lived by individuals in the moment, rather than about theory or skill. I continue to be deeply committed to valuing life in all its complex, contradictory, paradoxical reality and I believe that hazarding these personal observations, even if they are going to be scrutinized by others, is the only way to do justice to an approach that demands directness and courage. If we ask our clients to be open and self-aware, we must be capable of such openness ourselves. If we truly believe that life is there to be lived to the full, passionately and in all its intensity, then we should be pleased to take some risks and let others know of the dangers we have encountered on the way. To overcome the obstacles is always the objective, until we realize that it is the process of passionate overcoming, not the safety that results at the end, that is life's paradoxical joy.

I am deeply grateful to my parents, Anna and Arie van Deurzen, to my children Ben and Sasha Smith and to my companion Digby Tantam, for having been true and good when everything else failed. Their love is the light on my way.

Sheffield, September 1997

1

INTRODUCTION

Psychotherapy and counselling are professions that concern themselves with human dilemmas, human difficulties, human distress, human aspirations, human fears and dreams and many more such human pre-occupations. In other words, psychotherapy and counselling are about understanding the human condition.

The human condition is riddled with contradictions. We live in a constant tension between opposites, moving between wakefulness and sleep, confidence and doubt, belonging and isolation, sickness and health, life and death. As soon as we are born our future death becomes inevitable. Whenever things go well in our lives we become at once apprehensive of the next problem or catastrophe, which we know from experience might be waiting for us just around the next corner. Life is a constant cycle of ups and downs, of achievements and failures, of encounters and separations, of joys and sorrows, of hopes and disappointments. Exposure to these contradictions generates emotions that can easily swing us out of control. Life is an obstacle course for which there are no dry runs and about which we learn nothing if not through our own experiences and mistakes.

Much as we would like to think that people would consult a psychotherapist or a counsellor in order simply to get better at managing these problems in living, the reality is that people come to these professionals principally when they feel overwhelmed and out of control. They wait to get help until they are sinking, rather than coming in order to learn how to swim. People often come to counselling or psychotherapy because they need help in making sense of something strange or new. They are in the dark and need someone to shine a light in that darkness. They are lost and need to find themselves. They are down and need to climb out of their despair. They are confused and need to make sense of things again. They are in doubt and need to discover a new sense of purpose.

BREAKING AWAY FROM PATHOLOGY

There is a tendency in the field of counselling and psychotherapy to consider such moments of trouble and need for assistance as the consequence of some intrinsic personal problem, which can only be sorted out by an expert on the human psyche or on human relations. We seem to assume that people ought to be immune from the difficulties that their lives expose them to and that they should be able to cope at all times. We conclude that if they do not cope there is something wrong with them, rather than with the situation. We assume that what is wrong can be set right by some kind of curative intervention.

Counsellors and psychotherapists, however, soon discover that they cannot cure anyone of life. Life, as someone once put it, is a terminal disease which can only be remedied by death. Life is certainly not easy and there is nothing surprising in people finding themselves sometimes suddenly very much out of their depth. There are certain life events, such as immigration, bereavement of a loved one, loss of a job and many other sorts of losses, that can throw even the most balanced person out of kilter. There are certain accumulations of stress that can carry distresses beyond what one previously thought endurable. We cannot avoid the realities of human living, neither can we always bear them when they come. Life is hard and people are not always equal to its challenges. But life is also rewarding for those who are willing to put their shoulder to the plough and carry on regardless. Those who do so discover that they can develop new strengths and find new enjoyments.

FACING HUMAN DILEMMAS

Such enjoyment can only be found if we are prepared to immerse ourselves in life. Those who try to evade the human condition and who hide away from their troubles find themselves increasingly incapable of coping, because they become cut off and easily overwhelmed when things go wrong.

Cutting off from life is not a solution to dealing with its misfortunes. Yet immersing oneself in the flow of life inevitably brings the possibility of suffering as well as that of enjoyment. Counsellors and psychotherapists need to be prepared to work with this paradox. Counselling and psychotherapy, at least from an existential perspective, are about helping people in finding the courage to face their predicaments and struggles. They are about helping people to bring back some passion into their lives.

Paradox and passion are the bedrock and fuel of our work and it is by opening ourselves to their full impact on the client that new purpose can be generated and sustained. If the objective is to help a person get better at living, we have to be prepared to help them look at the way they live now in a radically fresh and revolutionary way. We cannot content ourselves with old fashioned interpretations. We have to set aside our personal and professional prejudice. We have to be prepared, as it were, to look life in the eye.

This isn't an easy thing to do, but then the predicaments that our clients bring to us are not easy to live with or to overcome. Psychotherapy and counselling are not about taking the easy way out. The paradox that should guide our work is that the more we engage with our difficulties and the more intensely we live, the stronger we get and the more satisfying life is. If we shirk and avoid facing reality, we become weak and soft and we live a life that is dull and full of denial.

Nietzsche gave us an interesting challenge when he said:

> My suffering and my pity—what of them! For do I aspire after happiness? I aspire after my *work*.
>
> (Nietzsche, 1883)

The work that this book speaks of is that of letting human paradox and human passion matter again. What is required of counsellors and psychotherapists who work from an existential perspective is to let all the intensity and all the ambiguity of life come to the fore. This book considers a range of topics, all of which are centred around the simple facts of human living. All of them are essentially concerned with the rediscovery and clarification of human dilemmas. They document my stumbling and humble search for understanding and truth.

2

PARADOX

ONTOLOGICAL INSECURITY REVISITED: SELF-CONFIDENCE VERSUS ANXIETY

> The individual in the ordinary circumstances of living may feel
> more unreal than real; in a literal sense, more dead than alive; pre-
> cariously differentiated from the rest of the world, so that his iden-
> tity and autonomy are always in question. He may lack the
> experience of his own temporal continuity. He may not possess an
> over-riding sense of personal consistency or cohesiveness. He may
> feel more insubstantial than substantial and unable to assume that
> the stuff he is made of is genuine, good, valuable. And he may feel
> his self as partially divorced from his body.
>
> (R.D. Laing, *The Divided Self*, 1960)

This definition of ontological insecurity from *The Divided Self* made a
tremendous impact on psychiatric and psychological thinking all over
the world. Laing's notion of ontological insecurity conjures up a pre-
carious universe that seems all too familiar to many of us. Although
Laing was describing the experiences of those often labelled as schizophrenic, the success of his idea of ontological insecurity was based not
on its utility as a description of a psychopathological condition, but
rather on the fact that ontological insecurity characterizes ordinary
human experience.

It is my contention that both Laing's popularity and his subsequent
battle with misinterpretation of his work were due to this original insight
and his misnaming of this insight. I suspect that Laing was not himself
completely clear about the existential ideas that underpin his approach,
and that his own psychoanalytic and medical background condemned
him and his followers to continue thinking in terms of pathology, even
when they thought they were rejecting it. It is therefore important to
reconnect the notion of ontological insecurity with that of existential

anxiety, and to show how Laing's work can be put to an enhanced use within a more explicitly existential framework.

Ontological Insecurity Defined

Laing held the view that people who experience ontological insecurity are hampered in their being in some important ways. He argued that such is the fate of those who end up with labels of schizophrenia and viewed this as caused by a lack of securing influences in childhood. In trying to find the cause of ontological insecurity, he turned to ideas such as Bateson's notion of the double-bind and concepts of collusion between some family members at the expense of others. He believed that such situations lead to anxieties which paralyse and terrorize the insecure person.

The insecure person suffers a threefold threat to his or her existence: engulfment, implosion and petrification. *Engulfment* is described as that terror of being taken over by another, being smothered and surrounded whilst losing one's autonomy and freedom to exist. It is the experience of being flooded and overwhelmed by the other's presence, certainty and security. It leads to a sense of having been driven into a tiny corner of living space. Laing (1959) gives the illustration of an argument between two psychiatric patients, culminating in the following remark:

> I can't go on. You are arguing in order to have the pleasure of triumphing over me. At best you win an argument. At worst you lose an argument. I am arguing in order to preserve my existence.
> (Laing, 1959, p. 43)

Implosion goes even further than engulfment, for here the inner vacuum is at risk of actually being filled by this external power. The concept is a stronger version of Winnicott's (1958) notion of impingement. As a consequence of a sense of inner emptiness the external world becomes a major threat: something that can burst in on one at any moment. One is, as it were, nothing but emptiness. External reality is the persecutor.

Petrification (or depersonalization) is in one sense a response to the dangers of engulfment and implosion, whilst simultaneously manifesting its own destructive characteristics. Out of terror one switches off and disconnects from the dangerous world of others and finds oneself in total stone-dead isolation. At a loss for sustenance, warmth or engagement with a shared human reality, one becomes depersonalized.

The ontologically insecure individual is split into a mind and a body. Being on the whole identified with the mind, the individual then becomes disembodied. Such a divorce of self from body deprives the disembodied self from direct participation in any aspect of the life of the world, which is mediated exclusively through the body's perceptions, feelings and movements (Laing, 1959, p. 69).

Personal Relevance of the Concept

These basic notions of Laing's and his deep understanding of the suffering involved in being human touched the imagination of many who read his books. While apparently describing schizophrenic, or at least schizoid, phenomena, Laing was, I suspect, describing his own experience and that of his readers, who perhaps recognized in these words the description of an existential predicament which they had often felt but had been unable to articulate.

This certainly was my own experience, as I discovered R.D. Laing's work at a time when I needed this acknowledgement of my personal struggle to find a safe place in the world. Like many others I felt a sense of welcome recognition and relief in reading these descriptions. Suddenly the fears and the loneliness that I had experienced in excruciating isolation were connected to other people's experience in a positive manner. I had previously been able to find only psychoanalytic theories to explain my unease and these inevitably portrayed me as immature, insufficient and pathological. I did not feel immature, insufficient or pathological: I felt heroic and special, engaged in a genuine struggle, even though perhaps a little weak, young and lacking in confidence.

It was in the early 1970s, as I worked in psychiatric hospitals in the South of France, that I had found myself resonating much more strongly with the psychiatric patients, especially with young schizophrenics, than with the medical establishment that looked after them. For some time this was of some concern to me—especially when a short spell of psychoanalytic therapy led me to consider my ideas about myself in pathological terms.

Fortunately, I was confident enough of my own sanity to conclude that there was at least as much madness in the medical establishment as in myself and the patients that I had begun to work with. I allied myself with the patients and began to try to understand why their beliefs were so obscured by both their own symptoms and the "cure" that was offered to them. Why did their truth turn awry and make them victims? Why did I find it so hard to speak my own mind on these issues when I was surrounded by members of the psychiatric establishment?

When I came across Laing's work it was like a flash of the blindingly obvious. I felt my struggles to be redeemed and my insights to have been vindicated. I gained the courage to speak as well as think my own thoughts. To this day I feel greatly indebted to R.D. Laing for having spoken up for me and having started the revolution in psychiatry that made independent and existential thinking possible.

Ontological Insecurity and Schizophrenia

It is remarkable that recognizing oneself in descriptions of schizophrenia can be so reassuring. What makes this possible, I think, is that Laing's sympathies obviously lie with "schizophrenia". In spite of his later denials of having idealized schizophrenia, there is little doubt that Laing felt that those people labelled schizophrenic often possess a heightened awareness of the existential dilemmas ordinary mortals tend to forget about. In *The Politics of Experience* (1967), for example, he writes that "even through his profound wretchedness and disintegration" the schizophrenic is "the hierophant of the sacred" (pp. 109–10).

Like Kierkegaard and Nietzsche before him, Laing gave a new dignity and respectability to those of us who resonate with the infinite at the price of not fitting into the normal social order. But then, ironically, he became the victim of his own courage when he was reproached for idealizing the suffering of the schizophrenic. He responded by retreating to a position of acknowledging this suffering for all the negativity he knew it only too well to contain. Because he had not separated the ontological insecurity and visionary capacity from the condition of schizophrenia, Laing had condemned himself to a position from which he could only speak for schizophrenia and anti-psychiatry, or indeed psychiatry, but not for life itself.

Anti-psychiatry and the Failure of the Concept to Thrive

Laing's contribution attracted many followers who were not challengers. Admirers came to live in the therapeutic communities that flourished around his new cult of the ontologically insecure. Whilst experimentation led to some new developments, the main thrust of much of Laing's early work was diverted and diluted. It was all too obvious that anti-psychiatry was not the panacea that it seemed to be in books like *The Divided Self.* Anti-psychiatry lacked the methodological and theoretical underpinnings that could have gained it a place in mainstream psychotherapeutic thinking. Little was offered (and demonstrated in practice) save for the proposition that ontological insecurity led to madness and chaos.

So, as time went by, Laing's promising beginning began to look like a flash in the pan and many of his followers turned to greener pastures, joining forces with the Kleinians, the Jungians, the Lacanians or the

Humanists. Laing had condemned himself to remaining a marginal figure; a mere guru rather than the potent and groundbreaking innovator that he seemed at first to be.

Therapeutic Communities and Insecurity

I recall my acute disenchantment upon discovering—at my own expense—that the magic of anti-psychiatry had sadly been replaced by bewilderment and confusion. The therapeutic communities that I came to Great Britain to work in had very little to offer apart from the claim to being safe havens away from mental hospitals. My experience of living in such a therapeutic community as a psychotherapist was that it deprived me of my role, function and professional dignity. It paralysed, deskilled and disempowered me. On a personal level it plunged me into one of the most nihilistic experiences imaginable. My ontological insecurity reached an all-time high.

It was a grim consolation that Laing himself seemed to fare little better, as he seemed engaged in battles with deep inner confusion in those days, during the middle and late 1970s. He appeared to have little of substance to offer in lectures and discussions and systematically discouraged my attempts at learning from him. I eventually contented myself with the lesson of my disappointment and concentrated on the discovery and depth of my own plunge into nowhere and nothing instead.

And so it was that, by offering nothing, Laing achieved my insight into what he had written about more effectively than if he had taught me any other way. For here was the experience at first hand: I once more felt the full blow of being an alien in a foreign country. I had given up my stable position for no more than insecurity and a handful of illusions, now all broken to pieces. And this time there was no professional identity to fall back upon: there was only closeness to those who themselves suffered alienation and insecurity to redeem me. It was the plunge over this precipice of anxiety and isolation that made me understand what ontological insecurity was truly about.

Ontological Insecurity and Existential Anxiety

I began to see how Laing had put his finger on the core of human experience, but had failed to see the value of this. Whilst people reproached him for having idealized the experience of the schizophrenic, I began to reproach him for having mystified the experience of ontological insecurity by linking it indissolubly with schizophrenia. To me, what Laing was describing was pure existential anxiety, but while Laing described the terror of existential anxiety as clearly as Kierkegaard had done a century earlier, he insisted on medicalizing it by tying it to a pathological condition. Instead of demystifying schizophrenia, this made schizophrenia seem like the equivalent of an LSD trip: a possible way out of the oppression of industrial, consumerist, post-modern society. To others it merely degraded Laing's theories, as he seemed not to realize that not all of us can afford to go mad. By equating ontological insecurity to the onset of schizophrenia, Laing had in fact achieved making existential anxiety more taboo, isolating it, as it were, in a psychotic ghetto.

The Object-relational Take-over Bid

Serious followers, however, could not just dismiss Laing's insights, which they recognized as holding some truth. In an attempt at getting out of the impasse that Laing's ideas seemed to have led them into, some tried to reconnect Laing's work with that of the British object-relations school of psychoanalysis, which already figured in his work through Winnicott's influence. Their laudable aim was to treat schizophrenia psychoanalytically and rescue people from the terrible ontological insecurity and abusive childhood experiences of which they had been victims.

It was this latter view that took hold, vigorously. In fact, it is a view that is still gaining ground in the therapeutic arena. Miller (1979), for example, bases her approach on the concepts of childhood abuse and trauma. Of course, such a position fuels the therapeutic industry, which becomes the only hope of rescue for the traumatized many.

The victimization of schizophrenics and accusation of the families that raised them has been a curse in our society for decades. What began with R.D. Laing's recognition of the gifts of the sensitive people we usually refer to as schizoid, turned into the commiseration with their terrible suffering and exposure of their parents' mistakes in bringing them up.

This trend has now spread to commiseration with those who have been ill-treated in any way at all. We are a long way from the existential notion that life is tough and that people can take much hardship in their stride. The picture is one of a perfect society where parents should treat their children with great gentleness and respect. Any shortfall to this standard supposedly leads to trauma and psychological damage.

The Existential Perspective

What has really become lost here is what made Laing's books successful in the first place, but what has perhaps never been made explicit by him or even truly understood by him, namely that the ontological insecurity at the core of schizophrenia is essentially there in all of us. From an existential perspective one would consider such insecurity and its concomitant existential anxiety to be the *sine qua non* of true vitality.

It is one thing to note that this resonance with anxiety can go berserk and lead to madness. It is quite another to forget that those who allow themselves the experience of such anxiety are often deeply engaged with the vital issues of life and death. When we read the passages in *The Divided Self* dealing with ontological insecurity as descriptions of our basic existential situation, rather than confining them to the experiences of schizophrenics, we may retrieve the original potency of their effect. For then we can also differentiate this essentially human experience of alienation from the ineffective response to that experience characteristic of schizophrenia. Laing's insights then become available to us without committing us to the worship of schizophrenia or the equation of every sensitive person's struggles with life with the onset of schizophrenia.

But this, as far as I am concerned, is precisely the problem with Laing's work. Rather than taking a radical and consistent existential position with Kierkegaard, Nietzsche, Heidegger or Sartre, arguing existential anxiety to be the core experience of being human, Laing reverts to the view that only some of us experience this anxiety. In doing so he ties the central experience of ontological insecurity to a pathological condition, instead of recognizing its essential and fundamental nature. It is this either/or, black/white position that deprives Laing's work of staying power. For him there is no other option: either we go along with the abject normality that our society and families try to make us conform to, or we revolt and become prone to schizophrenia.

The recognition that schizophrenics are often capable of more insight into the human condition than people who are well inserted into the established order is of course an important contribution. But this needs to be put into perspective with the complementary recognition that it is possible to have those same visionary or insightful qualities in a more creative way. The connections and differences between artists and schizophrenics need to be observed: it is not good enough to recognize the similarity between genius and madness: it is just as important to locate the essential distinctions.

What the two have in common is an extraordinary openness to the dilemmas of the human condition, coupled with a capacity to make unexpected links and observations. Such sensitivity can make it hard for a person to fit into ordinary hypocritical and secure functioning. But the essential difference is that artists, visionaries or geniuses are able to process and express these insights in some constructive manner, whereas schizophrenia is equated with feeling overwhelmed, oppressed and isolated by such sensitivity.

As I indicated above, I am myself no stranger to the experience of special sensitivity to the human condition and I have often felt different and isolated. It was important to discover how such a position could lead me into a dead-end street, even while valuing my own vulnerability. Laing's work provided me with a much-needed excuse for expressing my perceptions and experiences and believing in the rightness and rightfulness of such a position. But it wouldn't have been good enough to express my insights as a manifestation of schizophrenia: for that would have led me back to the same cul-de-sac.

When I came to England to work in an Arbours community, I still believed that schizophrenics and other visionaries just needed their special capacities to be acknowledged as such to keep them out of mental hospitals. But I soon realized that, for many of the people I encountered in these anti-psychiatric havens, even a medical approach would be preferable to the alternative that was proposed: that of stewing in apathy and confusion. All too often the well-intentioned community environment was inadequate in challenging the unease of the individual and merely confirmed a dependency similar to that found in mental hospitals.

Away from Pathology

I don't believe any longer that the equation of ontological insecurity with schizophrenia is helpful. Schizophrenia seems to me to be special sensitivity with quite a lot else on top. Experiencing deep sensitivity does not necessarily lead to schizophrenia and indeed could lead to a life lived with great insight and passion.

Equally intense experience of special sensitivity does not automatically lead to enlightenment. If one is particularly sensitive and one does not find an outlet for the great energies that become thus accumulated, it may well be that schizophrenia, or at least confusion and inability to function in the social world, ensue. In that case it is likely that one will need some very skilled and sustained assistance in finding a way forward again.

Schizophrenia may be the outcome of an extreme alienation and intense protracted exposure to existential anxiety (generated through special sensitivity). But we must not forget that such an experience is nothing more than an extreme form of the core human experience of being insecure: deeply and totally essentially insecure. To recognize such basic isolation and uncertainty can be the beginning of wisdom. It is the notion of ontological insecurity that forms the basis of existential philosophy.

The existential view expressed by authors such as Heidegger (1927) and Sartre (1943a) is that people have no solid self, no essential substance to rely on; they are basically pockets of nothingness. It is this essential non-solidity that makes freedom and consciousness possible in the first place. The price to pay for openness and flexibility is a deep-seated sense of vulnerability: ontological insecurity, experienced as existential anxiety.

The norm is to try to remedy the feeling of emptiness by filling it up with a semblance of substance. The aim of education and psychotherapy is often to help individuals achieve a feeling of security and confidence. A strong sense of self is supposed to be desirable. There is little doubt that apparently secure individuals function more successfully in a society which places great emphasis on self-aggrandisement and material acquisition. Experience has taught me that it is hard for a "secure" person to question these values and to pursue a policy of self-doubt and openness to the mysteries around one. Nothing is easier than to pathologize a doubting individual: nothing is easier than for such an individual to become convinced of his or her inadequacy.

Much of Laing's work aimed at finding the cause of such inadequacy in the pathological interactions within the family and within society. It seems to me that the so-called pathological interactions that he described in *Sanity, Madness and the Family* (Laing and Esterson, 1964) could also be found in countless families not affected by schizophrenia. The idea that their insecurity was caused by their parents' lack of consideration for them was so appealing to so many people that the studies were never checked or contested effectively. People all over the Western world felt justified in blaming their worries and weaknesses on the family they came from or the society they lived in.

So, from the recognition of our insecurity, we move to the consideration of such insecurity as a pathological phenomenon, to blaming it on our family and social nexus, to fearing that we may be schizophrenic. How about asking ourselves whether it may be a good thing that we are able to recognize our insecurity? How about the possibility of being grateful to our family for not having made us too complacent and leaving some gaps for our discontent and awareness? How about recognizing that there is a long way from rebellious insecurity to the alienation of schizophrenia? How about using these insights to help adolescents who are in danger of collapsing themselves into the trap of pathology when they are on the verge of awakening to the reality of insecurity and human sensitivity? Of course, one should not go so far as overlooking the fact that some forms of fundamental material or social insecurity are crippling, but the ontological insecurity spoken of here is on a different ideological and experiential level than the suffering of those who are deprived of basic survival needs.

My own experience in this illustrates the point. It was all too often tempting during my training as a psychotherapist to be drawn into the notion that my conflicts invariably stemmed from unhappy childhood experiences: it was easy to find much wrong with what my parents said and done and even easier to blame them for all they had not said and done. Although surplus insecurity may be generated by certain aspects of one's early (and later!) experience, many people find it reassuring to attribute all basic insecurities to pathological interactions with their parents and to hold that an adequate upbringing would bring about complete inner security.

The human desire for love and care is endless: our essential nothing-ness can never be filled up with enough attention, recognition or under-standing. No parents could possibly fulfil the heart's desires of any child: they will always inevitably and totally fall short of the ideal mark. In this sense, Winnicott's notion of "good-enough" mothers (Winnicott, 1958) and Bettelheim's extension of this into good-enough parenting (Bettelheim, 1987) are existentially more realistic than some of the wishful thinking in other theories.

One can spend decades retracing one's steps and looking into every nook and cranny of experience and still always find oneself and others basically lacking. The search for perfection is as much a consequence of the given imperfection that we have to cope with as the eternal dissatis-faction with this state of affairs. But what a relief to admit that one is basically and totally lacking: what a discovery to recognize that this is the very thing that one is, and that far from being a handicap this is the very thing that makes human life possible at all.

It is insecurity that spurs us on to explore the world. It is anxiety that allows us to not become complacent. It is coming to terms with this reality in oneself that makes it possible also to recognize it as it manifests in others. Perfection, no matter how desirable, is nothing but death: death is perfection. For it is only when we die that life is completed. While we live, life is imperfect and incomplete: it is this that motivates us to work and improve the world. Yet we discover that we always fail and that our efforts are inevitably insufficient and we remain insecure to the last.

Therefore, to come to terms with imperfection and incompleteness and to introduce one's children to it and help them to cope with it must be one of the main tasks in life. Helping clients to come to terms with the same paradoxes and tragi-comic flaws of existence is an essential challenge of existential psychotherapy. Exposing and getting used to ontological in-security and existential anxiety is the key to such an approach.

Conclusion

In order to get into the right spirit for this, the challenge is open to those of us who have adjusted only too comfortably to the status quo of a society that covers up our essential insecurity. We need to question and scrape away at the easy answers and expose ourselves to some of the anxiety that can bring us back to life in a real and deep way.

Daring to vibrate with ontological insecurity and recognizing it in others can bring some quite different discoveries than those of the experience of engulfment, implosion and petrification. It can shake us up and make us aware of our hypocrisies and duplicities. For when it comes down to it, none of us is really secure: social position, or material ease, or personal relationships may protect us momentarily, but a time might come when we get deprived of such advantages and find ourselves exposed and stripped to the bone—once more to experience the core of insecurity.

It is not, then, so much in order to understand, defend or rescue those of us who are schizophrenic that we may want to look again at Laing's categories of ontological insecurity, as to prepare ourselves for our own moments of insight and openness. As therapists this may remind us that the aim of existential analysis is never to make life seem easy or safe, but always to be ready for a little more difficulty and to encourage a new openness and recognition of insecurity. For to be able to stand in one's ontological insecurity means to be ready for adventure, it means to not hide behind the securities that protect us and that obscure the challenges that make us move forward. And when we are prepared to face such challenges we may find, with Nietzsche, that "what does not kill me makes me stronger" (Nietzsche, 1889).

It was, to my mind, to this kind of Nietzschian experience that Laing could inspire people. For all their 1960s connotations, Laing's words at the end of *The Politics of Experience* still carry the power they had for me when I first read them. It is those words that convey his true existential contribution to the smashing of false securities. They are worth remembering when we get too complacent:

> If I could turn you on
> If I could drive you out of your wretched mind
> If I could tell you
> I would let you know

In these words Laing shows quite clearly that he is not in favour of a dutiful object-relations understanding of how one could fit back into the norm and soothe one's ontological insecurity. He is wholeheartedly on the side of insecurity and praises it, rejecting a well-adjusted, normal but constipated mentality.

Many people made him eat his words and turned his theory on its head until it was little more than a new tool for the diagnosis of family disturbance. In his most recent work it became obvious that Laing was still preoccupied with the more mystical connotations of his earlier statements and that he was concurrently preoccupied with his own uncertainty about what he had contributed. Laing was very good at doubting and at his best when he did so.

Somehow I think that his report of a talk by Paul Tillich (Laing, 1985) sums it all up succinctly:

> Perhaps Paul Tillich went too far. He doubted even, when Jesus asked his disciples who He was, whether He knew Himself. Maybe He had no idea Himself who He was and was genuinely interested in hearing their views. The old lady sitting beside me turned to me when the lecture was over, almost crying, and said, "It's not fair for a man like that to come here and destroy the faith of an old woman like me".

Laing, like Tillich, had a way of destroying people's faith and making them think again when their starting point had become doubt rather than certainty. As far as I am concerned this is one of Laing's most fundamental contributions: to destroy ontological security whenever it rears its pompous head. He understood that fundamental paradox of human living: that for all its insecurity, life is better when insecure and lively than when secure and dead.

COURTING DEATH: ISSUES OF LIFE AND DEATH
The Idea of Nothingness

I have always been intrigued by the idea of death and can distinctly remember trying to grasp the notion of nothingness at a pre-school age, standing in the bathroom and watching the water go down the plughole. I remember how a little later, when learning to read and write, I devised various theories on what would bring a person's death about, and I wondered whether you might just die when you had used up the entire supply of words that I imagined was given to you at the beginning of life, rather in the way that a woman reaches menopause when her egg supply runs out.

I remember struggling with the notion of nothingness and discussing it eagerly with my mother around the age of seven or eight. As a committed theosophist she did not really believe in nothingness and she gave me the image of life spiralling on and on. I struggled to grasp the idea of what would be left if you took all that spiralling life away. But trying to speak of the negative nothing soon led me to the realization that none of my pictures of the void could possibly be accurate, as any thought or image of nothingness already represented a something rather than a nothing. It was gratifying when I discovered, ten years later, that I had in my thinking about this followed the same path as the great Greek philosophers Socrates and Plato (Plato, 1938).

The Connection with Religion and Mysticism

I was puzzled that my school friends did not have similar preoccupations until I became aware that they were often neatly held by the framework of Judeo-Christianity, in either Protestant, Catholic or Jewish form, the creeds within which they were, almost without exception, brought up. My parents, as theosophists, had taught me some things about those Judeo-Christian views of the world, but also some things about Hinduism, Buddhism, Sufism and other forms of religious thinking. The concept of reincarnation figured strongly in their worldview and I became quite captivated with some of the more imaginative and romantic perspectives on the afterlife. It was somewhat perplexing that these views were often in contrast and contradiction with each other. I suppose it led me to becoming prematurely sceptical about the human endeavour to explain the unknown.

It also made me extremely curious and rather anxious to explore these things further and, being a bit of a bookworm, I rummaged through my parents' library, which contained all kinds of mystical literature. Predictably, I was at first attracted to what was most crude and easy to absorb and before long I became a source of secret information for my primary school friends. I invited them into an exclusive society that had romantic initiation ceremonies and rituals and an improvised club house, concealed in the bushes of the North Sea dunes. I was keen to share my knowledge about the mysteries of seances, graphology, palmistry, astrology and other assorted occult practices, which were fairly taboo subjects in The Netherlands of the 1950s. I also became rather popular as a teller of ghost stories, especially in the dormitories on school journeys. I gained considerable gratification and self-esteem from this special and somewhat macabre identity.

However, as I was acquiring this dusky reputation, the parents of one of my school friends alerted me to the fact that my heretic practices would doom me to hell after my death. It was a threat that I kept to myself and was suspicious of, but which I nevertheless took to heart, being an impressionable and cautious child. The experience sped up the normal process of growing out of my desire to dabble in the occult. From adolescence onward I turned my attention to reading, and sometimes even writing, detective stories, until I discovered philosophy and developed a much more contemplative and private preoccupation with the unknown and with death itself.

Fascination with the Great O

It wasn't surprising that I should have this fascination with death for, being a tall skinny child, prone to anaemia and low blood pressure, I fainted fairly easily and it always seemed to me that I went on small excursions into death during these occasional black-outs. The sensation of the sudden blurring of vision, the rush of blood in the ears, the world spinning and then receding into the distance as I fell through a hole in my consciousness was an occurrence I became quite used to and that I somewhat perversely relished. When I had a bicycle accident at the age of ten and spent a somewhat longer time in a coma, I felt that I had finally completed a genuine trip to the land of death. It seemed to me that it was a good place to go, whereas life itself was fraught with such horrid things as hospital care, where needles, lying still on one's back and not being allowed to read, loomed large.

The prospect of death has remained in my mind as a friendly and attractive escape route towards the great O of oblivion ever since. This has anchored my life in the quiet knowledge of my readiness to go, providing me with a source of courage in the face of danger. When the land of oblivion acquires such attraction it can, however, also become the macabre object of desire at moments when life becomes too unpleasant and unsavoury. Over the years it has become evident to me that such flirtation with death has the potential of making me somewhat unfaithful to life.

My friendly familiarity with death was confirmed when my grand-mother died and she was given a splendid send-off. My image of her on her deathbed is that of her in her greatest beauty and calm. She seemed like a statue carved out of white marble, dignified, smiling and relaxed, all of her worries and tension eased away. She looked to me as if she had been transported to an other world of everlasting joy, from where she would forever look down upon me, benevolently. The room in which she was laid out was filled with the perfume of what seemed like an ocean of flowers, lilies, lilac and lathyrus, everything in hues of white, mauve and lavender, her favourite colours. It was my first vision of actual death and it was utterly appealing: she was like a saint or an angel and everyone tiptoed around the house in a new reverence that confirmed my impression that she had been beatified or even deified by death. She seemed to promise me, the youngest of her eight grandchildren, a special protection from the beyond and I promptly identified deeply with the little match-girl in Andersen's story, the poor waif who ends up being saved of her earthly suffering and deprivation by joining her sweet grandmother in heaven.

Pathology and Trauma

I certainly did not suspect that such happy fantasies might be excessive and it came as a little bit of a shock when they were branded pathological by psychoanalytic interpretations offered to me in later years. It did not seem right to dismiss my creative attempts at making peace with death purely as defence mechanisms. I was rather proud of my ability to welcome death, even though I had achieved it in the light of what you might refer to as traumatic experiences.

The fact that my father had serious asthma, which became a life-threatening condition through severe pneumonia around the time of my birth, must surely have had something to do with my fascination with death. Throughout my childhood I frequently heard him fighting for breath, nearly choking to death on several occasions. Such observations would certainly have been quite likely to make me fear death, but to find a way out of that fear by making friends with the beyond to me seemed of the order of achievement rather than of the order of defence.

The reality was that my mother nursed my father back to life from his pneumonia just after I was born and this undoubtedly did contribute to introducing me to the battles of life and death at a pre-verbal level early on. Perhaps I even learnt that it was possible to be faced with such challenges and emerge from them intact. That would certainly have been confirmed by my experience of both of my parents often speaking to me about the dangers, deprivations and life-threatening experiences that they had been through in the Second World War. I was the willing audience to the accounts of their suffering during the Dutch winter of starvation in 1945. They had only just survived their ordeal by eating tulip bulbs, whilst my father remained hidden in the rafters of a freezing cold attic, expecting to be found and killed by the Germans at any time. They impressed me with a strong sense of the fragility, hazardousness and potential injustice of human life.

Even so, I would forcefully reject the view that such experiences traumatized me and induced a death-wish, which I then defended against. I am particularly sceptical of the suggestion that I became self-destructive out of a sense of guilt to be alive, or because I sensed that I was the cause of my father's illness. Both of these interpretations were offered to me at different times and they mostly served to dramatize my experience, colluding with a self-pitying stance which could have trapped me in the role of victim, making me all the more dependent on the analyst.

Death as an Adventure

The truth is that my original interest in death can be simply understood in the light of my early encounters with it, leading to a need to come to terms with it in a meaningful way. The meanings I have been able to attach to it myself are never final and they have been altered as I have understood more about myself and the world. The meanings attached to it in dogmatic ways by well-meaning therapists have sometimes clouded the waters and created disturbance. The therapeutic obsession with capturing other people's experiences in pre-set frameworks of meaning and interpretation can be truly destructive. My fascination with death was the equivalent of my ex-husband's childhood fascination with herpetology, which emerged because he was exposed to a rich Floridian fauna from a very early age and had the temperament to research and experiment with that. Making phallic and Oedipal interpretations on that score would not only rob him of his ability to have his own understanding of what it meant to him, but might also distort and falsify his commitment thereafter.

Similarly, when I had an accident at the age of ten this was not, in my view, because I acted out the unspoken parental aggression against me or because I was parasuicidal. I had an accident because I was adventurous. I got hurt because I was accustomed to exploring the world rather further afield than other children. My earlier fall from my mother's bicycle at the age of two, which also led to concussion, was a consequence of her adventurousness. The fact that I experienced concussion a third time when I was 16 and crashed my motorbike does not need to be seen as repetition compulsion or as more evidence for self-destructiveness. To me it merely exemplifies the theme of adventurousness and risk-taking, of getting into things, quickly and slightly prematurely. That trend appears throughout my life and inevitably leads to a small crash now and then. It is also the source of most of my pleasure and all of my achievements and I have accepted it as my hallmark, thereby freeing myself from crippling and demeaning interpretations of pathology.

When I think back to my early accidents I now feel a deep gratitude to my parents for having been able to accommodate my need to venture out and roam freely, in spite of the insecurity about my well-being that they had to suffer as a consequence. They could so easily have caged me in, forcing me to retreat inwardly. Instead they let me explore and learn for myself about the limits of my abilities and the risks on the road of life. In this way I acquired an early, visceral knowledge of the simple truth, that those who go out to travel the world encounter danger. My accidents and brushes with death were to me the only tangible proof of my independence and a small price to pay for it.

Rites of Passage

It is important to note that at this stage I was not seeking death, I was only interested in establishing what it was and where it belonged in relation to me. I was, in other words, exploring the boundaries of life. I was seeking to live life intensely, fully enough to also know about death. This confronted me with the question of what one does with the knowledge of danger and the awareness of the limits of existence. For having arrived at this point there is a choice between respecting the boundaries and retreating into life or diving ever deeper into the exploration of the mystery of death. The latter can become very appealing if death seems the only, or the most accessible, inroad into the unknown.

There can be little doubt that I gained much from my accidents and fainting spells, if only just the knowledge of how to guard my life more carefully. In addition, there were secondary benefits, including time off school and street-cred with my friends. Mostly it gave me a sense of being able to survive and stand the dangers of the world out there, even if getting injured sometimes. I knew that I had lived and survived and that I was solid, flexible and rugged: this gave me a blueprint for a mixture of confidence and prudence, which I like to think of as realism.

My little skirmishes with death were my rites of passage, my litmus test of life, my fire-branding, my initiation into adulthood. The scars that these experiences left gave me something by which to measure my maturity and stamina. They were concrete proof of my ability to survive, they were hard evidence that I was alive. Heidegger's descriptions of Being-towards-Death do far more justice to my experience than other interpretations. He speaks of the way in which the anticipation of death brings one face to face with the possibility of Being itself and he calls it: "Impassioned freedom towards death—a freedom which has been released from the illusions of the 'they' and which is factical, certain of itself, and anxious" (Heidegger, 1927, p. 266).

Death and Aloneness

This draws attention to yet another dimension of what I experienced in my encounters with injury and death. In becoming alerted to the precariousness of my own life, I was urgently confronted with my aloneness in the face of threat. When in hospital at the age of ten I felt utterly isolated and deprived of my mother's constant care, which had always been there as a safe haven to rush back to. I went through a state of emotional shock and a process of sudden awakening to the fact of my basic aloneness, and I experienced this as intense anxiety for many months after my body had recovered.

At 16 my concussion led to a similar rush of anxiety, but this time coupled to an urgent longing for aloneness and a need to retrieve myself and celebrate the new sense of identity that was emerging from my adventure. In the many weeks that I stayed in my bed at home, I had the time to linger in a new, rapidly evolving world of music and poetry, discovering myself. Each time it actually seemed as if the concussion had broken open a new part of my brain: almost as if a veil was being lifted and I could see more clearly both into myself and into the world.

Of course, these experiences are easy to idealize and they certainly gained increasingly positive significance as nodal points in the fabric of my life over the years. As I chose to dive into these experiences as a way of coming to grips with the challenges of living and dying, they assumed a quasi-religious significance. They were the occasions that drew me out of my shell, shook me out of my security, forcing me to take heed of life in all its challenging reality. They were stressful and painful events, which I then exploited as opportunities to get a special grip on life. They were the distinctive times that gave life new intensity, like the rapids that revitalize and cleanse a river, pulling twigs out of the slow and dull festering water close to the bank. I was sucked into the fast stream of life and surged into the flow of cascading living.

Risks and Dangers

It was exhilarating and bracing to be so immersed and to discover my vitality, personhood and capability. But there was a real risk of the flow of life submerging me, pulling me down a vortex. I came close to being flooded and inundated several times between the ages of 17 and 25. Before I learned to swim in the flow of life, I very nearly drowned. I believe it behoves me to talk of this experience of being drawn into death, because I think it is a real problem for some of us who work in this field. Our eagerness to explore the beyond leads to a friendly familiarity with the shadow side of life, which can lead to us being dragged down into the depths.

These opportunities to emerge into the wilder currents of existence constitute a true potential health hazard. I have sometimes wondered if there isn't a process of addiction at work, where the thrill of exposing oneself to deathly danger becomes a habit, without which it seems difficult to survive or thrive after a while. Some of us can be a bit like parachute or bungee jumpers. You can detect this attitude of commitment to perilous living most clearly in Nietzsche, for instance in his words in *Twilight of the Idols* (Nietzsche, 1888), where he incites us to bravery and where he makes the claim that "what does not kill me makes me stronger", as quoted above.

Nietzsche seems to imply that everything that is difficult and coped with makes you stronger, and that nothing can ever make you weaker. There is a kind of existential machismo here, which supposes that we become free through resolutely facing up to death. This stance is, of course, also prevalent in the early Heidegger (Heidegger, 1927). It is an attitude that can be extremely appealing, especially for those who are enduring hardship, but it involves a wishful denial of human frailty and of the process of decay and decomposition that can undermine our bravery. It is important that we should be willing to be somewhat wary of this glorification of stoicism and idealization of death, toughness and madness in the existential literature.

Therapeutic Tunnel Vision

Existential therapy, in common with most other forms of psychotherapy, tends to focus on the suffering and difficulties of life. But whilst other therapeutic approaches view such difficulties as abnormal, pathological or at least undesirable, existential therapists tend to consider them inevitable and sometimes, as I have just illustrated, they tend to see them as particularly desirable and virtuous. Instead of trying to rid humanity of anxiety, existential psychotherapists invite people to rediscover their anxiousness, anguish and dread and face up to it as part and parcel of their being-in-the-world. Although this is seemingly the opposite of normal therapeutic practice, it is arguably nothing but the other side of the same coin of *reductio ad traumatum et absurdum*.

Both classical and existential therapeutic practice is fixated on death, disease and trauma and only differ to the extent of considering these to be either proof of weakness or of potential strength. In becoming so well acquainted with death, we end up considering it the be-all and end-all of life. The question is whether this is a revelation of truth, as we tend to think, or whether it creates a distortion and a bias in our perspective on the world. It is undoubtedly more reassuring to think that my skirmishes with suffering and death are a sign of special merit, than to think that they are a sign of pathology, but in both cases I am missing out on some vital awareness of the demands of life.

I have come to believe that such encounters and tribulations are signs of neither pathology nor health. They are neither vice nor virtue, but quite simply an inseparable part of our route through life which needs to be put back into some overall perspective. The extent to which we experience such events ultimately as success or failure depends to a large extent on how well we know the territory we are exploring and how good we are at extricating ourselves from some tricky cul-de-sacs that we may get caught up in on the way.

Getting Caught in the Maze

Existentialist literature and philosophy often have the function of revealing these mysterious routes in the land of life and death and I certainly felt greatly heartened in my teens, when I discovered that there was instruction to be had in the art of finding your way about in life, by turning to the great authors, as I have said elsewhere (van Deurzen-Smith, 1989) and shall discuss in a later chapter. Existentialist literature in particular enlightened my own quest because it resonated with my experience and was the explanatory system that came closest to giving a flattering account of my world. The fact that this literature established death as the hub of the wheel of life was satisfying to me, because it corresponded to my personal version of the truth. The circularity of finding a theory that confirms your views and then using the theory to prove your intuitions is a common and satisfactory mode of operating in the human sciences. It may be the best we can do as long as living is to a large extent, as Spinelli would say, a matter of interpreting reality (Spinelli, 1989). This circularity becomes problematic, however, when it leads to a situation where the swirling of concepts leads to a downward spiral, which attracts one inward and downward with irresistible centrifugal force. This can occur if there is no longer enough challenge to one's beliefs and theories, a situation that we often set out to achieve so as to avoid discomfort. It happens particularly when a given notion is temporarily extremely successful in explaining reality.

Psychoanalysis is again a good example of this: in the wake of Freudian interpretation, everything one did or said could suddenly be explained from a drive perspective. One's words and actions appeared suddenly to all have sexual connotations and could be interpreted as evidence of one's libidinal and unconscious impulses. Such a totalization of experience can have a paralysing and counterproductive effect. We are suddenly caught in an explanatory system that drags us down and that exercises a kind of intellectual terrorism over us. Popper would accuse such theories of being non-falsifiable and therefore scientifically unsound (Popper, 1962).

Going Under

Existential thinking is often in danger of a similar non-falsifiable preoccupation, not with sex but with death. Such a fascination can be evidenced by a simple word count of key words throughout the existential literature from Kierkegaard to Yalom. The present chapter is a further case in point. It is undoubtedly an illustration of existential irony, or evidence of the paradoxical nature of life, that the approach is named after existence rather than after death. Perhaps we should consider referring to ourselves as thanatologists or restyle ourselves as necrophiliac therapists.

My mocking and perhaps even bitter tone at his point is related to my having come to question my own preoccupation with morbidity, as I have seen clear evidence of it leading to an impasse. I have begun to wonder whether I have spent rather too much of my life getting ready to die and not nearly enough of it savouring living. I chose as a personal motto, "memento mori" (remember that you'll die) at the age of 12. The fascination with death became more and more intense by the year as I came to grips with the demands of intellectual and scholarly pursuits and discovered that some of the greatest human accomplishments and feats of culture were centred around the acknowledgement of death, human tragedy and suffering. Sophocles, Shakespeare, Goethe, Mozart, Bach, Brecht,

Da Vinci, van Gogh: there are endless examples of how culture feeds on a continuous diet of distress and despair.

Of course, there were excursions into other kinds of flirtation, but for a serious-minded and passionate person a broken heart is the predictable result of an exclusive teenage love. A broken heart can lead straight back to a preoccupation with death, especially when the world around one is demonstrably decadent and morose. When wars are being fought every-where and pictures of broken lives and destruction stare at you from every newspaper, when the planet is getting harder to live on because of pollution and overpopulation, there can be few more gratifying projects than the pursuit of rebellious and devoted dissolution of self.

The Fight for Survival

So from the candid, adventurous, accidental confrontations with death of my childhood, I came to the pursuit of death as the way out towards a better world. The suicide attempts I played with when I was 17 were teenage despair turned to a longing for oblivion. There was still a kind of positive exploratory side to it, which I recognize in the drug addiction or self-mutilation with which so many young people experiment nowadays. But no 17-year-old takes tablets or puts her head through a noose for the fun of it, and there is no doubt that I was extremely tired of living. I thank my lucky stars that it was the plaster in my ceiling that crumbled, instead of me. The tablets merely made me sleep for a long time and I did not need hospitalization. What mattered was that when my parents dis-covered me to be too drowsy to go to school the next morning they took the time off to talk things through with me, themselves, instead of send-ing me for professional help. The Principal of my high school similarly rose to the occasion and enlisted me to tell him about the woes of my generation, encouraging me to help him to make reforms in the school. I felt acknowledged in my suffering and treated as if I had something to contribute because of it.

The poems and songs that I wrote as a result of my experience were published in the school journal and I had a go, with some of my friends and with the support of a favourite teacher, at putting together a rather daring and controversial cabaret. It ran for days on end with great suc-cess, both in our own and other schools, and got us acclaim in the news-papers. I discovered that I was creative and had something to offer to the world and so the world suddenly was worth living in again. It was very simple. Had I been treated for my depression, then my sadness, *Angst* and *Weltschmertz* would have been blown up out of all proportion. I doubt whether I would have emerged stronger out of that.

I don't believe in God, but I miss him.
Julian Barnes

26   PARADOX AND PASSION IN PSYCHOTHERAPY

The narrow tunnel through which I went in the 1960s to find a place in the adult world seems to have narrowed even more for children who grow to adulthood in the 1990s. Death is omnipresent in films and in the media. Images of hell these days relate more to life than to death, with fewer and fewer people believing in an after-life. There are now few images of terror spoiling the prospect of merciful oblivion and life can easily lose its power to please and appeal. Visions of the possibility of a successful life, filled with love and happiness, are becoming more rare and implausible. Instead, young people are faced with disillusionment and spiritual impoverishment as they are exposed to an initiation process of fierce competition for a place in the world, a job, a home and a partner. It is a process that all too easily leads to a loss of self-esteem and a sense of degradation.

Death as the Object of Desire

It seems as if we are now well beyond the Nietzschian observation that God is dead. In the process of killing God, we have also killed the godlike values in society. When God is dead, God equals death. Death, in other words, becomes the new God of the age. We are well beyond Heidegger's era, where it was possible to put Being in the place of God. Believing in an essential entity of Being is just as taboo and impossible in a post-modern society as believing in God. In our materialistic culture the ultimate is a belief in the void. Fate and chance seem to be the logical backdrop to the principles of evolution and growth that we have pinned our faith on. It is no wonder that we turn to such things as chaos theory and genetic engineering to give ourselves a final desperate boost of self-esteem and the illusion that we can control our destiny. The fact that we are no longer really fooled by our own prowess and that we are all too aware of the limits of all this human posturing is abundantly clear from popular literature, music and cinema.

After decades of emphasis on human achievement and personal will, the laws of harmony, care, intimacy and co-operation have been rather trampled on and life itself is left stranded and undervalued. One can observe the spreading despair of those who are faced with the prospect of having to carve out a life in a hostile society, where many can do little more than merely fight for personal survival. The fabric of society is increasingly taut and there is evidence in the figures of crime, suicide, alcoholism and drug-addiction that more and more people pursue a path of destruction or self-destruction.

As Kierkegaard (1855) said in *The Sickness unto Death*, "When death is the greatest danger, one hopes for life; but when one becomes acquainted with an even more dreadful danger, one hopes for death". Berdyaev (1948) expressed what many these days feel even more strongly when, in his book *The Destiny of Man*, he said that "Death, the greatest of evils, is more noble than life in this world". Nietzsche (1887) understood why this should be so for people who had killed God, and in *On the Genealogy of Morals* he asserted that "Man would sooner have the void for his purpose than be void of purpose".

I believe that Nietzsche hit the nail on the head in relating people's preoccupation with death to a lack of purpose and meaning. It is when one feels deprived of access to life, of an essential right to breathe and to speak and to think and to be, that one focuses on the void and on oblivion and on the black hole of death. It stands to reason that when the stars can no longer satisfy us with their light, we turn to the stars' destruction as our object of interest. This does not mean that it isn't a perfectly good and important subject for study, but it does create a distorted and biased focus, in the same way in which the elimination of death as the object of study also keeps us in the twilight of incomplete knowledge and understanding of the whole of what is.

Life and death are the two sides of one coin. They cannot be had without each other, they should not be kept apart and in isolation. What the existential approach does is to focus on the missing part of the puzzle, counterbalancing the scientific preoccupation with what is concrete. Whereas science investigates all that is positively there, existential thinking allows for the attention to be shifted to what is not in evidence, to what is in doubt and to what is absent. Existential thinking continuously hints at what is beyond the horizon of our ken. In doing so it runs the risk of becoming death-absorbed. By exploring the shadow side of existence, we may lose sight of the brighter sides of reality. Moreover, by dwelling in these mysterious places of darkness, we may go a little bit pale and lose out on the invigorating rays of living sunlight that are essential to our survival.

And this is where it gets serious: in courting death and other sinister sides of reality, we may find ourselves doing more than just exploring or discovering reality. It may well be that we create a deathlike universe for ourselves in the process, missing out on the nurturance and essential uplifting that is the *sine qua non* of living. Like spiders we weave our own webs to live in, we create ourselves and our environments as much as we are created by them, and by grasping on to death and destruction we are instrumental in influencing our own ecosystem in a morbid fashion, drawing an ever tighter circle of nihilation around us.

Deconstruction and the Dissolution of Self

I am no stranger to this self-created purgatory. For after surviving my own half-hearted suicide attempt and having proven my stamina by succeeding in my final exams, I struck out on the road towards what I imagined would be freedom and independence in the south of France. There I studied philosophy and became, rather predictably, more and more absorbed by the kind of intellectual despair and nausea so well described in Sartre's books. I had gone well beyond a desire for suicide, but I still did not think that life was so great. I had, of course, given up all the warmth with which my family and friends had surrounded me previously and I lived a rather lonely and isolated life. The world, in this different culture, seemed a hostile and absurd place to be. Realizing my need for commitment and human warmth I threw myself into my relationship with my new boyfriend and we moved in together.

Meanwhile, my studies in philosophy, psychoanalysis and Marxism taught me to be increasingly cynical and sceptical. I was instructed in the art of deconstruction, questioning the ideals and beliefs that I had previously held dear. Soon there was nothing left to hold on to, everything appeared as illusory, fake or bourgeois. In this sombre atmosphere I proceeded to get deeply involved with my boyfriend's medical studies, which seemed to offer a more constructive approach to life and I began to accompany him in his placements in various hospital departments.

Being exposed to the death of others in a concrete way, rather than to merely thinking about the abstraction of death, came as a shock to the system. Cancer wards, with their smell of decay, were deeply unsettling and changed the golden image of death as a portal to the afterlife into the notion that death is when the body rots. I was even more shaken by my experiences in the casualty department: for here people's bodies did not even have time to come to terms with life and the process of slow decay: here I was faced with people who met death violently and without any possible justification.

Facing the Reality of Death

One particular Christmas is especially engraved in my mind, as the time of a marathon encounter with would-be revellers, drunk drivers and victims of motorway pile-ups, brought in on stretchers in all states of distress and destruction after nightly car crashes. The eerie atmosphere of high-voltage tension, smell of ether and lights too bright for comfort, still lives on in my memory as the epitome of nightmare. I would return home in the morning in a state of shock and find it impossible to forget the distressed faces and torn bodies that I had seen. I am at times still disturbed, several decades later, by the image of a particular girl of 20, my own age at the time, livid as a ghost, lying stark naked on a hospital bed surrounded by machines and doctors in white coats. She was being administered a gruesome, last-resort, exploratory brain examination, which misfired whilst the machines were making a hellish noise and even the most composed medics looked tense and overawed by their inability to save this icon of life that should have blossomed but was fading fast. The carotid artery collapsed during the examination and blood spurted from the girl's neck over her pale waxen body, red on white, in a violent forceful fountain of useless life energy asserting itself in a last effort to repair her broken and shattered body.

I was not protected by the professional mantle of being doctor or nurse. I was merely a little foreign philosophy student, risking myself through identification and intense observation of the human tragedies played out in front of me. After a year of this intense exposure to the bleak world of death, on holiday in what was then Yugoslavia, I fell deeply ill with a raging high fever, vomiting and diarrhoea and fast loss of weight. After three weeks, having been transported back to the soaring heat of the South of France, I was hospitalized in a state of exhaustion with suspected leukaemia and my mother was summoned to take the first aeroplane from Holland to sit at my deathbed. It was only after days of hourly blood tests that it was declared that I was free of leukaemia and must have some infectious disease. No infectious disease was ever diagnosed, although there was some talk of scarlet fever. My body was so weakened that I had to relearn to walk when I came out of hospital. Once again I had narrowly escaped death. This time I had not liked what I saw at all. My fascination with death was definitely over and I merely wanted to live and relieve my own and others' misguided attraction to death.

Emerging into Life

I embraced life in a much more determined way from this moment on. I got married within months and moved to live and work in a radical and progressive psychiatric hospital in the Massif Central. I devoted myself enthusiastically to psychotherapy, finishing my philosophy studies with a dissertation on solipsism and schizophrenia, then studying psychology, writing a dissertation on attempted suicide, shifting my focus of interest from an obsession with death to a preoccupation with understanding why and how the will to live can break down.

My training in psychoanalytic psychotherapy and my work with psychiatric patients convinced me that a person's greatest risk of alienation lay in isolation. Professional commitment was one way out of that danger. The more professional expertise and social status I gained, the better my grip on life. It seemed as if I had finally discovered how to live, how to make a living for myself and how to convince myself that life was worthwhile. My grip on life was, however, entirely predicated on helping other people get a grip on life. After five years of this devoted life I sensed the hypocrisy of being a helper in a white coat, whilst all of my sympathy was with the patients that I tended to and who poured their troubles out to me. I had to put myself to a further test and this is when I came to England to live in a therapeutic community, allegedly to work at the cutting edge of my profession, but somehow, more truly, in order to see how good I really was at surviving life without the safety net of the hospital ward and the white coat.

On the Edge of Life

I must add that I was terrified to take this risk, giving up the security of a fairly settled professional life and a pleasant house in the south of France. I must also add that I would not have done so if it weren't for the fact that death spurred me on yet again. Within a matter of one year a number of catastrophes had struck my then husband and myself. First, my husband had been involved in an accident in which a two-year old girl was badly injured, leaving us standing mortified over another fragile and comatose life in a hospital. A few months later we witnessed a second traffic accident, which led to the death of a teenage girl, right in front of our eyes, when she was mown down by an oncoming truck. We naturally took charge at the scene and stood by her as her brain spilled over the tarmac and we had to admit defeat in the face of death. In spite of surface cool and professionalism, calming a bystander's hysterical attack, stopping the traffic, assisting the fire-brigade, I had been stunned by the impact that the participation in violent death still had on me, in spite of all that had gone before. The sight of her split skull and torn leg will be forever at the back of my mind.

But the third disaster, somehow prefigured by these events, was the worst and consisted in the discovery of the dead, stiffened, poisoned body of the dog that we had loved like a child. All of this happened against the background of our fight against infertility, which had culminated in our certain knowledge that we would never have children. It felt as if there was nothing left to lose and so we came to London to work and live with other people who had nothing left to lose, only to discover that you can always lose even more.

Suffice it to say that my life was shaken to its core by trying to bring myself out of the complacent and artificial identities I had acquired over the years. I abandoned my French nationality, also temporarily my professional status, and finally my marriage. I let go of all that had given me so much security, but that now seemed wrong-headed and ruined. I had a final fling with total freedom, absolute love, utter devotion and the exploration of what lies in a land beyond reality.

I discovered in a final and very concrete and complete way that absolute love or absolute anything equals death. Death is not just the unknown over the horizon, neither is it merely pure oblivion: death is what you move towards when you plunge totally into yourself, away from the distractions and commitments that keep you realistic, alive and in a functional state. Sartre may have dismissed such illusions as "bad faith", but it may be that our greatest peril is to discard this vital process of illusion formation.

Choosing to Live

Being pragmatic and rational, I understood that I would destroy myself if I ventured any further or any longer into such a state of pure freedom and love. I did not want to die, I had seen enough of death by now to want to save it for later. I wanted to live and discover the secrets of life as I had discovered the secrets of death. I hoped that I could transmit my love of life to those who had brought me to this new edge of existence and I flattered myself temporarily with the idea that I was indeed doing so. Eventually I had to learn the lesson that life can not be transmitted unless others are willing and able to receive and sustain it for themselves. I finally had to face the sober and sordid facts of life alone without further drifting and dreaming towards perfection and oblivion.

I gave myself a chance to live for real at last and entirely under my own steam. When I had completed my sense of being able to sustain myself, no matter what the challenges and in spite of considerable loneliness, I knew I was ready to find someone who could do the same and who would wish to be alive and create new life with me. Fifteen years on, we had children, a house and pets and books and courses and mutual respect and support and love and affection, together with the whole exhausting and difficult daily struggle that comes with life. I wouldn't have understood what it takes if I hadn't taken the time to experiment with living and dying as I did.

I am finally beginning to get more at ease with life, trusting it to be basically sound in spite of all its adversity and imperfection. I learn daily lessons in accepting my own fallibility and smallness, no longer striving for holiness, purity or an ideal world, just doing the best I can. Somehow I found a place in the world where I can create some being out of nothingness and it doesn't matter to me so much now that I, like everyone else, live on borrowed time and with lots of illusions.

Accepting the Paradox

A preoccupation with death is still there, right at the core of me, but I am in no hurry to find out more about it, just now. Death or nothingness seems like a steady hollow presence somewhere at the centre of me. I don't have to fear or to court it, because it is an intrinsic part of me and it is what keeps me open to life. With the years going by it becomes easier to give in to it, as it is beginning to manifest itself inexorably through the wrinkling of my skin, the greying of my hair and the slowing down of my metabolism as I grow older. It is a strange comfort to be so mortal and moved by time. It is rather nice to make friends with the kind of gradual death that gnaws away at us all and to have the patience to wear myself out, using myself up one day at a time. It is teaching me to monitor carefully how I use my energies, whilst having faith in the slow cooking process of maturation and decay. I experience a growing joy in the release of not having to chase after death, but letting it slowly bubble up in the pot of life instead.

I am not exactly sure any more why I had this frantic fascination with death so early on in life. It occurs to me now that it was a kind of wild and untempered yearning to merge with the universe. It was an energy of life that wasn't sure that it had a place to go and a right to be, an obsession with retrieving life from the edges of death, so as to hold it close and possess it. My courting of death was an impatience: a wanting to get to the end of the book, to know the outcome of the story. But I found that by reading the final tragic chapters before knowing the characters well enough, the book of life itself became distorted and eschewed, losing its appeal and ability to enchant.

I submit that wanting to possess the book of life is a symptom of our times, where life has become harder to relish and savour, having been deprived of its mysteries. Those of us who feel impelled to make a difference to the world and to not squander ourselves, may falter when we find ourselves continuously disowned and disenfranchized. We compensate by grasping the whole of life as an idea instead of living it, and we end up believing that we can control life somehow by loving death.

A rather pompous doctor of my acquaintance once claimed that people were so impressed with the medical profession because doctors are the only people who have access to life and death. I argued with him that priests are more qualified to hold this function because doctors merely attend to the processes of life and death, trying to coax them into submission, whereas priests witness the realities and significance of these processes and are meant to guide people through them. Becoming an existential psychotherapist was the closest I could get to being a secular priestess.

Hard experience has taught me that priests and priestesses, even existential ones, may know rather little about life, unless they are willing to be drawn into it themselves. I now believe that there is a group of people better qualified than others, not through professional knowledge, but through biology, to claim an intimate knowledge of the transitions of life and death. Of course I am referring to mothers who, having given birth, understand exactly how mysterious life is and how close it is to death, the fear of which is always at the horizon when you have a new-born baby in your arms. But more than anything motherhood has demonstrated to me that it is labour and hard work alone that keep life alive and death at bay. The challenge of keeping life afloat is an absorbing and demanding project. Addiction to the thrills and spills of death anxiety, death provocation and death flirtation are hazardous sports that seem to lose their appeal as soon as one has sunk one's teeth into life itself, that is in the labour of living the ordinary everyday.

The Labour of the Everyday

The daily routines of caring for and with others is what lends real lustre to life. Discovering that such care is mutual and therefore potentially co-generating is a strangely underrated yet hardly well kept secret. It is noteworthy, though, how little existentialist authors seem to know about it. Like the poets and the artists, they swoon over the drama of life and they fail to notice that the ordinary existence of ordinary people is cut of an entirely different cloth. I know the attraction of the stark world of the tragic, but it may be that we do our clients a disservice by ignoring the much softer call of the ordinary life with others.

For existential work to come into its own we need to go beyond the Heideggerian and Kierkegaardian obsession with death, traverse the desert of deconstructionism and plant the seeds of a new living understanding of ourselves which leads to a respect and welcoming of life. I don't think there are shortcuts and I believe that the road towards such understanding must cross self-doubt and death often enough to be at ease with it. Some of us, however, get somewhat distracted when looking death in the eye too often. We need to guard against an obsession with death and bring ourselves back out into the light, daring to seek and affirm life.

Confronted with the fire of our battles with death and anxiety, we need to remember that we are not salamanders or phoenixes and that only mythical animals do not get burnt to a crisp. A little less heroism and a little more lightness in admitting defeat can lead to greater strength and more good cheer than a sad and sullen martyrdom. Some have suggested that we need the courage to live (Tillich, 1952). Others have suggested that we need to face death in order to find such courage (Yalom, 1980; van Deurzen-Smith, 1988). Perhaps what we are missing in all of this is the appeal of life itself, the gift of life that is already ours to make the most of. Our Christian brethren and sisters call it "grace" when we open ourselves to receiving this gift of life. This has moralistic implications, particularly by suggesting the use of the word "disgrace" for those who disdainfully refuse the gift of life. Heidegger, of course, sought to provide us with an existential alternative to this concept and he spoke of "releasement" (Heidegger, 1954) to counterbalance his original emphasis on resolution (Heidegger, 1927). But Heidegger's releasement is more like a final letting-go and does not capture the process of give and take, which leads to the discovery that when we truly give to life, without fear of annihilation, we get replenished for free.

Into the Future

I have not, as yet, found any convincing descriptions of how to be a flexible vehicle for life: most attempts are too self-absorbed or goal-orientated. I am as curious now about discovering more about what makes life flow freely as I was puzzled by what might lie beyond death 25 years ago. I have found existentialist literature not nearly as capable of informing me on this matter as I found it informative on issues concerning suffering and death. I don't think that many psychologists, analysts or philosophers have captured what the subtle secret of a life well lived really is. Their explanations sketch out some of the mechanics of living and most of its pathology, but remain silent on the actual fabric of life as it is experienced by those who live it carefully and with relish.

My observations of my own clumsy attempts at living are only a very modest start to my new project. There is much to learn. My days of courting death are over. I am ready to start courting life a little more. The life I mean is not the opposite of death. It is the fullness of bios, which includes libido and thanatos amongst many other factors. I know that my new courtship requires from me a new light-heartedness, a playfulness and a sense of humour. It requires me to take myself a lot less seriously and life a lot more easily.

Maybe one could argue that all this is just a sign of my growing older, maybe it is also a sign of the times. It doesn't really matter. Whatever the reason or the explanation, it feels like a homecoming and it is restful and loaded with promise. I shall relish this new ripening of the tree of life. I know it will bear fruit some day. Meanwhile I shall patiently wait and watch, carefully observing and taking heed. If there is anything to report I shall speak up. But it may just be that what I discover is something that cannot be said at all. In that case I hope that I shall be able to follow Wittgenstein's (1961) advice and that I shall be wise enough to just keep silent.

THE SURVIVAL OF THE SELF

In this section I shall consider how we establish and maintain a sense of self in relation to an outside world which demands our participation in it, often to such an extent that we get taken over or absorbed by it. I shall ask whether there is such a thing as a self to start with, and if there is, whether it is in danger of extinction. I shall refer to the post-modern assertion that self is illusion and investigate the implications of such a contention for psychotherapy. I shall then look at the themes of participation and power in relation to this new image of the self or absence of the self. As you are reading this, you may want to participate in the investigation directly by thinking about your personal observations of your own experiences of selfhood. The objective is to come to some useful conclusions about the interplay between self and other, between individual and group. This may give us some pointers towards the survival of the self in a world that poses such constant threats to it.

Classical Concepts of the Self

Concepts of self vary tremendously across human history and culture. The range spans from Christian images of an immortal soul to the Buddhist belief in selflessness. In Western thinking the notion of self has been debated by philosophers from many different perspectives. Hume's *Treatise on Human Nature*, for instance, observes that:

> I never can catch myself at any time without a perception, and never can observe any thing but the perception. When my perceptions are removed for any time, as by sound sleep; so long am I insensible of myself, and may truly be said not to exist.
>
> (Hume, 1739, p. 252)

Strangely, such explorations of the fragile basis of the self are often ignored by psychologists and psychotherapists, who tend to make the self into a central concept, creating the illusion of its substantiality. In psychoanalytic literature Freud used the term "self" as mainly equivalent to "ego". As Hartmann (1956) has pointed out, prior to 1923, Freud used the term "ego" (das Ich) to refer to "one's own person". Federn (1953) described the self (ego) as the felt sense of one's own existence. Winnicott (1965) distinguished between the true and false self, describing the latter as "the inherited potential which is experiencing a continuity of being, and acquiring on its own way and at its own speed a personal psychic reality and a personal body scheme" (p. 46). Jacobson (1964) followed leads from Hartmann and described the self as one's self-image.

More recently, the self psychologists in the USA have particularly concentrated on the concept of self. Kohut (1972), for instance, contrasts two views of the self. One is the self as a content of the mind and in the other, the self is seen as: "the centre of our being from which all initiative springs and where all experiences end". Kernberg (1980), following Fairbairn (1952), whom he describes as the most profound of the British middle group, characterizes the self as the totality of self representations in relation to the totality of images of others. Both these authors believe that self and other images are inseparable, which brings us back towards questioning the independence or substantiality of the self.

Such questioning is also present in continental Europe, where the influence of the psychoanalytic theories of Lacan have been dominant for some decades, with the view that the self is fundamentally a lack which desires to be filled. Lacan's views are related to existentialist thinking as well as to the more recent movement of post-modernism, which denies the possibility of the existence of a self altogether.

R.D. Laing, who could in some ways be seen as the point of contact between the school of object relations and that of existential psychotherapy, grappled with similar notions. He introduced a concept of self which was always at risk of being taken over and harmed by the outside world. As he describes the delusions of schizophrenics, he argues that these contain existential truth and that for these people:

> The self is probably conceived as immortal or made of nearly imperishable non-bodily substance. He may call it "life substance" or his "soul", or even have his own name for it and feel that he can be robbed of it.
>
> (Laing, 1960, p. 149)

As usual, Laing's statement has a prophetic quality and concerns quite a bit more than the plight of schizophrenics. He is speaking for many people today who feel that there is a danger that their very selfhood, the core of their being, might be taken away from them. This theme was taken up by authors such as Lasch (1984) and Barrett (1986), who claimed that Western culture poses such a threat to human individuality that the experience of loss of self is omnipresent. It may be that we have reached an age of such nihilism, that the very essence of our personal being is undermined.

The Existential View of Self

This links directly with the views on selfhood that were arrived at by existential authors, particularly by Heidegger and Sartre, who both denied the concept of a substantial self as it is often taken for granted by psychotherapists. Sartre's view (1943a) is that the self is something that is artificially generated out of a fundamentally open consciousness, which at first directs its attention towards the world without any sense of self-consciousness as it is mere intention. We are at this time only vaguely aware of being the source of our perceptions and impressions. It is only after others comment on our behaviour and way of being in the world that we begin to build artificial notions of having a self. We create a self out of others' perceptions of us. This self becomes more complete when we discover the possibility of actively determining the direction of our actions. By projecting ourselves into the future we develop confidence in our own existence. Eventually we may become capable of achieving a sense of embodied self, where our bodily awareness of being a centre of consciousness coincides with what we do in the world, in past, present and future. Sartre considers this establishment of selfhood a goal rather than a birthright. It is not something that a person ought to achieve by a certain age in a normal developmental process. Neither is it a particularly desirable objective, for the creation of a self concept is part of what Sartre terms "bad faith". Bad faith is the attempt to act as if one is solidly constituted as an object. To be like an object is to have an essence and a clearly designed role and function. Human beings do not have such an essence or defined function. It is their role in life to be free and to discover their possibilities and limitations and to bear the uncertainties and conflicts that come with this freedom.

Sartre's work was much inspired by Heidegger's original challenge to the notion of self. For Heidegger (1927) there is no self, only being-in-the-world, a process of connecting to the world that we are thrown into. He distinguishes between inauthentic being, which is the mode of being when we persuade ourselves of the necessity of various things and when we let ourselves be taken over by others, and authentic being, which is what we become capable of when we realize that we are transparent consciousness which inexorably moves towards death. To give up the illusion of self-aggrandisement and solidity that comes with inauthenticity leads to a sense of insight and openness that allows us to reveal truth instead of pursuing various external objectives. According to Heidegger, it is our task to become capable of such exposure of what is, in reality, and let the world and being become manifest through our lives. This is not about strengthening or asserting self but rather about leaving ourselves open so as to become able to reflect Being (Zimmerman, 1981).

These concepts of transparent or non-self are hard to take on board. They are not unlike Buddhist notions of selflessness and they leave us wondering how to conduct our lives in relation to other people and the demands that society makes on us. We can ask ourselves, in particular, what happens to participation and power in the context of selflessness? Before moving on to that point you might like to take a minute to ponder on your own sense of self and how it is interwoven with the world around you. If you wrote down ten quick definitions of your self, without thinking too much about it what would they be?

Looking at your definitions you can ask yourself which of them belong in which categories of human existence. Firstly, there may be some that are related to definitions of your body (I am a woman, middle-aged, tall, thin, etc.), then there will be some that will be definitions of your social role (I am a mother, a wife, a lecturer, a keen dancer), thirdly there may be some that define your character or personality (I am active, thoughtful, resilient, intense, etc.) and finally there will be some that describe your beliefs and values (I care about the health of the earth, I aim to be truthful, I am a committed existential therapist, etc.). Ask yourself how many of these aspects of yourself are absolutely intrinsic to you and how each of them could be questioned, undermined and taken away again. How do you normally conduct your life in such a way as to reaffirm and repeat these aspects of you that you experience as constituting the self that is you?

The Self as a Process rather than an Essence

According to existential philosophy, such confirmation of specific aspects of yourself is a form of "mineralization": a process of reification of what is, in principle, malleable and flexible. It is an attempt to think of yourself as just so, when there are in fact many alternative ways of moving forwards into the world. What we call the self can be seen as no more and no less than a person's centre of gravity. More recently, Dennett (1991) has spoken of the self as a centre of narrative gravity. This centre of gravity is first and foremost situated in the body that we are. Yet we may, as it were, reach out of our body towards the world and our centre of gravity will inevitably become unbalanced in this way. It can therefore be located differently according to the way in which a person extends into the world and in relation to how much room he or she has been able to make for him- or herself in that outer space that we stand and move in. Our centre of gravity is altered as we enter into contact with the world and it may be totally unbalanced when we have to disconnect suddenly from outside relationships that we can no longer maintain for one reason or another.

This is when we realize how little of ourselves we really can take for granted. When I lose something or someone dear to me, I feel empty. I feel lonely and hollow when I am let down. It is perhaps particularly at these times, when I am at my low ebb, that I can really see the stuff I am made of, or rather that I can almost tangibly perceive what I am not. I am not opaque and solid. I am not made of the things that I usually hold so close to myself that they become me. I am instead an empty space, a vessel that can be filled and emptied, according to the times and tides of man. I am a source and a medium, not a thing, not a substance, not an entity in my own right.

What I let myself go into, get absorbed in, becomes part of me, becomes me, temporarily. I adopt things from the outside world in order to create a sense of fullness and avoid the openness and hollowness that is me. I could in principle remain flexible and open to adopting different aspects of the world all the time. In practice, people usually recommit themselves daily to the same sort of things, ideas, people, notions, concepts, beliefs, memories, as the day before. If I do this I create a kind of continuity for myself. I have a set pathway into the world and therefore I become associated with that particular pathway and the mode of being it requires of me. I may even end up believing that I am this continuity, that these properties that I cultivate in order to be in this modality are actually what defines me: this is when I can truly say that I have created a self. It may be that such a concept of my self is, however, essentially illusory and can be undone quite readily through loss of the habitual pathway.

When I speak of illusions in this context I do not mean this in a deroga-tory way. I believe this process of making the world our own, of connect-ing closely with others, with roles, with certain images of oneself and with certain ideas about the world to be indispensable to our survival. The illusions of substantiality of our self that this may create are, however, an unnecessary encumbrance which complicates our lives.

Interaction between World and Self

Although we ourselves may not be as substantial as we once liked to think, we still find ourselves at the centre of our consciousness. The balancing act that we all have to work with is that of going out towards the world whilst maintaining a centeredness and equilibrium at the core. In terms of human relationships, this leads to the experience of the polar-ities of belonging and isolation, dominance and submission, power and impotence, contact and disconnection, recognition and rejection, particip-ation and avoidance. We are inexorably bound to others, as Heidegger observed, and inter-subjectivity is one of the givens of a human existence.

To be able to participate in the world is the *sine qua non* of living, but this very act of going out to be part of the world also endangers us and it needs to be counterbalanced by a movement towards the centre of gravity that we ourselves constitute. Some of us seek out the dangers of fusion and belonging more than others, some of us are better at managing the hazards of the journey out there in the world than others. Some are more active about encountering the world, others wait for the world to meet them. Many of us struggle with the finding of a balance between immersing ourselves with public levels of participation in society or with another person whilst maintaining a sense of inner integrity. I would like to illustrate such struggles with some examples taken from my professional experience, before I ask you to dive into yourself and remember your own struggles with participation and withdrawal, power and impotence. This may allow you to get a better grasp of the volatile and fragile process of establishing and expanding an inner centre of integrity that can withstand increasingly greater assaults upon it.

Our challenge in relation to others is twofold. It is played out both in the public domain of our participation in large organizations and in the private domain in intimate relationships with significant others. Both of these are relevant and I shall consider them in turn.

Public Relationships

Recently I had the experience of allowing my sense of selfhood to become taken over by an organization for which I worked voluntarily. I found that the more energy I put into it, the more absorbed I became by its contradictions, which gradually began to define me as a person. In an attempt to bridge these contradictions I ended up feeling torn to shreds by warring factions. I discovered that there are certain modes of participation in power that cannot be withstood with any sort of integrity because the forces of organizations are eventually greater than that of any individual. Participation in some of these forces is not conducive to the sort of self one might like to foster.

If selfhood is not a set thing, but is rather constituted of what one associates with, commits to, attaches oneself to, singles out, absorbs, concentrates on, then it matters tremendously what one opts into, whom one belongs with, what one concentrates one's energy on. It is not a simple matter of voluntarism, although the will to get things right can make a difference between going under or surviving, between being taken over or trying to change things that are not right. There remains a matter of whether one is able to accommodate what is there in one's environment and purify poisonous elements sufficiently through one's system to come out alive and strengthened rather than weakened and harmed. Integrity is only maintainable within the limits of what one can tolerate and eliminate, all of our personal systems are fallible and there are limits to what we can absorb, digest and eliminate.

Power corrupts, which means that we become so associated with forces stronger than ourselves that we forget to account for our own actions. Absolute power corrupts absolutely, and absolute participation in the public world of politics similarly can take one over absolutely, making it apparently unnecessary and indeed impossible to realign oneself with personal concerns. The group can take over from us and determine our actions. We become absorbed by the law of the group that we belong to and become determined by its principles and direction.

As I go out into the world, I jeopardize my inner balance. My centre of gravity becomes redefined by what I reach out towards. In relating in a certain way and addressing myself to certain aspects of the world, I exclude other ways and aspects of myself. I push myself forward through a certain channel, a certain lens, a certain sieve of reality, and the response I get determines my own answer. Most of this happens in action rather than through a process of reflection and choice. I vote with my feet and immerse myself in the world. Then it meets me and feeds me certain information, certain moods, certain realities that I then have to integrate, work with and respond to, for better or for worse.

Perhaps you can think of a situation in which you have become aware of letting yourself be taken over by a group, where your involvement in an organization or some public cause has led you to wonder how you could retrieve yourself from the dictates and pressures of the group before you would go under and lose your sense of balance. Ask yourself how you succeeded in retrieving a sense of personal self that allowed you to survive with dignity and integrity. How did you manage to re-emerge from this organizational take-over?

Personal Relationships

After reflecting on your own balancing act in relation to the public dimension you might shift your attention to the more private aspects of negotiating a sense of self. Some of us avoid confrontation with the more intimate aspects of relationship altogether, but most of us spend a lifetime struggling with the push and pull of belonging with another whilst maintaining a sense of autonomy as well. The movement from dependency to independence via counter-dependency may eventually lead to mature inter-dependence, but this assumes the predictable course of an essential self. If our selfhood is rather more transparent than objectrelationists think, then it is far less surprising that so many never master the delicate balancing act that is required of us in maintaining a sense of self, whilst being drawn to others.

An example of this is that of my client, Rosa, who came to me when she was struggling with a strong infatuation which had taken over every aspect of her life. The man with whom she was in love was married and she spent much of her time fantasizing about what it would be like if he left his wife and moved in with her. Most of her actions were geared towards persuading him to love her more. She felt as if she was only alive when he cared about her, as if the world was exclusively constituted by his presence and destroyed by his absence. She had gone out of herself to him so far that her inner centre of balance was precariously teetering on the edge of disaster. If he did not call her when he said he would, usually for a perfectly good reason, she felt threatened to the extent of becoming unable to function. When he could not see her for more than a week, which happened often because of his work and family commitments, she thought that she was dissolving into nothingness. Her being had no reason other than being for him. If he did not want her she would literally "go spare": all of her would seem like excess existence, for which there was no need and no reason to exist.

Rosa had been an independent woman for over 15 years. She had, after a divorce, lived by herself happily, whilst being successful in her job and having occasional intimate relationships with colleagues and friends. She was quite taken aback at finding herself so much at this man's mercy and could not herself understand what had happened to her. She felt the need for him as so essential that it was like the need for water when thirsty. Previously she had always felt a great sense of reserve when in an emotional relationship with a man. She experienced this need as positive on the whole, as it had opened her to a sense of yearning for life that made her feel more real and more vulnerable, allowing her much stronger experiences than she had ever had before. Yet, this gave her lover more and more importance in her eyes, as he alone was capable of satisfying this craving, and he became associated with long-awaited moments of gratification. The man in question was apparently astounded at the role she had assigned him and he accepted to play it to the extent that was convenient to him, which on the whole was insufficient to satisfy her need, therefore keeping her waiting and longing much of the time.

Rosa saw herself as extremely generous in the relationship: generous with her time, her devotion to him, the presents she gave him, the love she made to him, the availability of herself that she offered him. She felt that he did not appreciate this but took her for granted and, in a sense, this was all that she felt that she was entitled to expect. It was all part of the scenario of sacrifice that she had set up for herself and her love for him thrived on it rather than being destroyed by it. Rosa did not complain of her predicament, as she valued her love for this man more than she resented the suffering that it demanded of her. She even valued the suffering, which she felt was purifying her, making her into a better person. It was not Rosa's objective in therapy to rid herself of this obsession, but rather to understand what it meant to her and what it was that she was gaining in the process of extending herself so far towards another human being. This she did very successfully and, as her commitment to this state of unbalance became an accepted fact of her everyday existence, she felt that her need for this man subsided whilst her sense of her own ability to shift her centre of inner balance from him to her and back again increased. In the end she felt able to accommodate the most extreme extensions towards this other person, whilst being able to recover an inner sense of completeness and centeredness when he was not available to meet her. It was this sense of expansion of herself that made the need for him wane somewhat. She valued her new-found strength in being able to stretch so far beyond herself with so much self-contained certainty that she could recover herself again no matter how far she had moved towards him.

Rosa's experience is a good example of how the obsession with another person may be put to good use, rather than be lived as victimization. It was Rosa's act of redefining this experience, as one of getting to know herself as a new person, that allowed her to stop suffering. In essence, Rosa reinterpreted her experience of selfhood as encompassing all the extremes of ups and downs, all the oscillations between aloneness and fusion with another. She had to re-situate herself as a person capable of such breadth and flexibility and find peace in inhabiting a new universe, which was sometimes filled with glorious togetherness and at other times restricted to the narrow confines of her sorrow. When she learnt to accommodate the enormity of such experience, accepting it as all part of her, it stopped being torture to gain and lose her lover all the time, for in losing him she no longer lost herself. In practising the art of extending herself in this way, Rosa discovered that she had broadened her basis of existence and that she had managed to achieve a better balance in every other aspect of her life through it. Her previously rather more narrowly defined sense of self was abandoned. Rosa spoke of having risen like a phoenix from her own ashes. She felt that she had survived the death of her former self.

As you ponder on Rosa's experience you might like to take a little time to reflect upon your own struggles to maintain yourself within an intimate relationship. Is there a time when you had to relinquish control and with it a sense of your own sense of self? How did you handle this? Did you find yourself collapsing into confusion and despair? Did you let the other take you over and show you the way? Did you fight or avoid the other out of fear? How did you eventually manage to find a new sense of self in relation to this other?

Conclusions

There is much food for thought when we begin to face up to our own lack of certitude about having a solid, definitive and reliable sense of self. Psychotherapy becomes a lot less of a certainty too, if we have to accept that the person may be a rather more fragile entity than we always assumed.

Laing's notion that psychotherapy is a re-search for all we have lost (Laing, 1967:47) becomes very poignant in this light. If we are capable of constantly losing ourselves, then psychotherapy may be a never-ending search for the self which ultimately always defeats its own purpose. If we can hold on to our own experiences of losing ourselves and retrieving ourselves anew, we may become capable of reading less pathology into our clients' accounts of themselves and have more empathy with their struggle to survive.

INTIMACY: CLOSENESS AND DISTANCE BETWEEN SELF AND OTHER

Meeting in Groups

When we meet in large groups we sometimes do not meet others at all, because we feel too threatened by all these people around us. We may spend much of our time trying to be good enough to be accepted by the group or otherwise trying to hide ourselves away because we do not think ourselves good enough. We may be so successful at hiding that we end up not only hiding from others but hiding from ourselves as well.

Groups that are aware of the risks of such avoidance and alienation may attempt to create structures and modalities that enhance intimacy. However, such attempts can easily backfire. If I get drawn into doing specific exercises to meet others and expose myself, this may constitute such a threat that I learn to pretend to be intimate and open whilst actually hiding behind the mask of this fake intimacy and feeling even more alienated than before. Trying to break down barriers may create new, even tougher barriers. Now I may not even realize that I have barricaded myself behind apparent ease and sharing of intimate details.

What is Intimacy?

It is useful to ask ourselves the question of what others represent for us and how we relate to them and what we really want from them. It is well worth asking the question of what intimacy really is. Rather than thinking that we already know what intimacy is, and rather than assuming that it is always a good and desirable thing, we need to learn to question such a concept. What about the intimacy we do not want? What about the intimacy that is not appropriate? What about the intimacy that is fake?

We need to ask ourselves what role intimacy plays in counselling and psychotherapy, as these professions are essentially based on the use of an intimate relationship and often aim to enhance a person's capacity for intimacy. So let's begin to examine the issues a little more closely and turn to some people who have thought deeply about these matters long before us. T.S. Eliot struggled with these questions and he put it like this in his poem, "Little Gidding":

Who then devised this torment? Love.
Love is the unfamiliar Name
Behind the hands that wove
The intolerable shirt of flame
Which human power cannot remove
We only live, only suspire
Consumed by either fire or fire.

(Eliot, 1944a)

We have to love. We cannot avoid it. We are all thrown into this world together with others, whether we like it or not, and it matters to us what they think about us. Heidegger (1927) said that one of the fundamental aspects of being human was to care about things and be concerned about others. There is no way out of this torment and often we experience others as our tormentors. Sartre suggested that hell was other people (Sartre, 1943a, b). What he meant was that we do not need to devise an image of hell other than that of being alive in a world where we make things difficult for each other because we all have clashing objectives and get in each others' way.

Problems in Communicating

Clients often come to us because they feel tortured about caring for others or because they do not know how to care for others. They may also be worried about others who care for them too much or too little. Problems with human relationships overwhelmingly dominate the exchange between counsellors, psychotherapists and their clients. Clients come to counselling or therapy to learn what is possible in human interaction and they come to learn it in practice, through the therapeutic relationship itself.

It is important not to assume that people want intimacy or should want intimacy. It is far safer to posit that people are essentially ambivalent about human relationships. We all are fated to have to find our way in this world with other people. We can't avoid others and we need others and yet we sometimes like to think that we are autonomous and can manage without them. Much of the current therapeutic culture is about teaching people to be self-reliant, self-assertive and autonomous. Our clients crave the ideal of independence, which seems to hold out the promise of freedom of the burden of human relations. Many of us have intensely mixed feelings about this whole business of intimacy. We certainly do not want to be intimate all the time and certainly not with everybody. Some of us would rather not be intimate at all. When we relate to others we often play complicated games, checking out whether we can trust the other to be understanding enough to get a little closer to them and at the same time withdrawing again to a safe enough place that leaves us relating in a more conservative manner.

Louis MacNeice put it very well in a poem called *Conversation*:

> Ordinary people are peculiar too:
> Watch the vagrant in their eyes
> Who sneaks away while they are talking with you
> Into some black wood behind the skull,
> Following un- or other realities
> Fishing for shadows in a pool.
>
> But sometimes the vagrant comes the other way
> Out of their eyes and into yours
> Having mistaken you perhaps for yesterday
> Or for tomorrow night, a wood in which
> He may pick up among the pine-needles and burrs
> The lost purse, the dropped stitch.
>
> Vagrancy however is forbidden; ordinary men
> Soon come back to normal, look you straight
> In the eyes as if to say "It will not happen again"
> Put up a barrage of common sense to baulk
> Intimacy but by mistake interpolate
> Swear-words like roses in their talk.

(MacNeice, 1949)

MacNeice has understood something very important here: that we cannot afford to reach out too far and that it is safer and more realistic for us most of the time to stay at a comfortable distance from each other. At the same time he notes that we bridge this distance all the time by such commonplace things as swearing. We reach out to others with ourselves through our emotions and by using certain words rather than others. We give ourselves away all too often without doing so deliberately or without necessarily overseeing the consequences of our actions. We reach out to each other because the urge for communication and a sharing of what we have in common is even stronger than that for independence.

Speaking to Each Other

If we were content to be independent and autonomous all our lives, then monologues would be all that would ever occur. And surely much of our so-called human interaction is actually based on a juxtaposition of many monologues, hardly reaching into each other's hearts and minds at all. But when interchange begins to happen, in ordinary conversation, that to which I would refer as "duologue", i.e. a time when two people speak with each other, there are moments when it is evident that there is more between us than just talk, just facts, just an exchange of information or just two people posing or pretending to relate. Of course, there are many times when people limit themselves to merely speaking in monologue to the other, following the simple trail of their own words and not bothering about the effect on the other or rather trying to steer clear of being interrupted or influenced by the other's words or attitude in return. Duologue takes such separate speaking one step further as people come together and begin to interchange with each other. But just talking to each other and at each other in this kind of dual monologue does not make a dialogue.

Martin Buber put it so wisely:

> The most eager speaking at one another does not make a dialogue—
> for dialogue no sound is necessary, not even a gesture.
>
> (Buber, 1929, p. 3)

To achieve dialogue and true conversation, instead of merely that of a double monologue, i.e. a duologue, we need a little more than eager relating and speaking to each other. Do you realize what the word dialogue actually means? It comes from the etymological root "dia", which means "through" and "logue", which means "to reason or to speak". To dialogue therefore literally means to reason through something, or to think through something with words. It is a process a bit like that of dialectics, which comes from the same root: a posing of one idea, opposing it with another and then finding the synthesis that can overcome both ideas and take them further, to the next idea, which itself will create a new opposition and synthesis, and so on and so forth.

We notice in the first place that by this definition dialogue does not need two or more participants: dialoguing might indeed be done alone. Secondly, it does not automatically come about when there are several people speaking to each other. It may in fact be that where people come together there is a tendency to not think through things with words, but rather to exchange words of monologue, in an attempt to hold one's own in the face of the other.

True dialogue, according to Buber (1929) does not come about from retreating into mystical silence or some other form of superior relating. True dialogue requires us to open ourselves inwardly for the other person. What we have to do is to lift the spell of fear between people. We do this by going out towards the other.

> He releases in himself a reserve over which only he himself has power—no more knowing is needed. Where unreserve has ruled,

even wordlessly, between men, the word of dialogue has happened
sacramentally.

(Buber, 1929, p. 14)

When I move out towards the other, giving up my reserve in myself, I
do away with the usual moulding and fabricating of attitude and
appearance. I let go of a sense of superiority or inferiority: I stop comparing myself to the other or trying to create an impression or preoccupy
myself in any other way with my effect upon the other or the other's
effect upon me. Instead, I devote myself to making myself as transparent
as I can: not any longer standing in the way of the encounter and not
attempting to be more or less than I am. Instead of wanting to be something I allow myself to be a vessel for the meeting with the other and I
move out of my shell into the open field, where I can meet the other and
be ready for whatever is to come.

Gabriel Marcel used a lovely phrase to indicate the sort of availability
that was needed to achieve the right mode of encounter, he called it "a
mutual availability for what the future holds in store" (Marcel, 1935). This
indicates very clearly how, in true dialogue, I place the emphasis neither
on you nor on me, but rather on what binds us together, on the space that
we have created between us. What happens between two people who
stop hiding from themselves and from the other in such an unreserved
encounter is that they come together on the ground that is situated in
between them, where they share a common humanity. Buber used to
speak of the in-between as the ground of the encounter (Buber, 1929).

When I put myself at the service of my clients from this perspective I
achieve a twofold movement away from self-absorption and away from
client-absorption. I am no longer self-centred or client-centred. I am instead centred on what lies between us. On the one hand I become aware
of what the other brings in terms of our shared humanity and I can get a
bird's eye view of it and see it in perspective. On the other hand, and at
the same time, I recognize some of the same issues that I grapple with for
myself and I discover our shared human condition, even though it is lived
somewhat differently by each of us.

As a therapist or counsellor this is the challenge that I have to put to
myself. To find a new facet of the condition that I already have experienced for so many years from my own angle and perspective in the story
and experience of each and every client. Their predicament is always
mine, in some form or shape. It either already has been mine, is now, or
will be in the future. Nothing anyone experiences is ever totally alien to
me and I encounter the other as a companion on the road of life and with
a fascination for their particular view on it. What I can learn with them
about the predicament that they are in is both familiar and new, always

adding a new dimension to what I have seen before, and yet it is never more than just one more piece of the same old puzzle.

Two is Company

Herbert Read put it into words in relation to his experience of the men under his command in the war, those who were both his companions and yet also men he had responsibility for. In his poem, *My Company*, he said:

I can assume
A giant attitude and godlike mood
And then detachedly regard
All riots, conflicts and collisions.

The men I've lived with
Lurch suddenly into a far perspective
They distantly gather like a dark cloud of birds
In the autumn sky.

Urged by some unanimous
Volition or fate
Clouds clash in opposition,
The sky quivers, the dead descend,
Earth yawns.
They are all of one species.

From my giant attitude,
In godlike mood,
I laugh till space is filled
With hellish merriment.

Then again I assume
My human docility,
Bow my head
And share their doom.

(Read, 1946)

I am both above the condition of humanity that these others are drawn into and very much a part of it. I can remove myself from entering into the other's world by keeping a sense of godlike overview, but in the end I can only enter into true dialogue with others if I am willing to bow my head and share their doom. I am no more and no less than others. Others are in the end nothing but the reminder of myself and of the possibilities or catastrophes that I may encounter. Others are there as companions and brothers and sisters more than as allies or enemies. The task I have when I relate to you is to bring myself thus into our shared life so that something new, something worthwhile, can be created. I receive in return for what I give to my encounter with you the same new vigour and nurturance that I contribute. What I give is what I get.

In true dialogue, both of us bring our personal views to the exchange between us and we put these at the disposal of our shared attempt at widening our vision. In dialogue I come forward with my given thoughts and give them new thought, taking my ideas forward. My focus is on the problem, the issue at hand, rather than on you or on me. If you do the same, then between us the issue receives full attention and neither you nor I stand in the way of clarifying and understanding it, putting it into its right context and place, until obstacles are overcome and contradictions resolved or put back in their correct order.

Between us something has melted away in the process; instead of fission we experience fusion. In the space between us we have created through our diversity and difference something new that neither you nor I alone could have envisaged in isolation. Our separate perspectives form the backdrop for a new, grander design. Our separate realities, brought together, throw a new light on a shared and more complex reality: together we can begin the work of dialogue—the working through with words of whatever issues are at hand.

As Buber said: the world calls out to us and the presence of others addresses us and calls us to come out of ourselves to each other. Buber used to speak of I–It and I–Thou relationships and he believed that there was no such thing as a separate I, but only the I of the I–It or the I of the I–Thou (Buber, 1923). We become partial and like an object when we relate to the world or the other as an object in the partial way of the I–It. We become complete and an individual when we relate to the world or the other as a Thou. The way in which we relate is also the way in which we make ourselves into one or the other: an It or a Thou. We make ourselves partial or complete in the process of relating to others in a partial or complete way. We cannot be in I–Thou mode all the time, for life in the world sometimes requires us to be partial and objective. But we only fully come to life when we relate to the totality of what is, and for Buber this meant to relate to God, through the world or the other in the I–Thou mode (Buber, 1923).

Implications for the Therapeutic Relationship

Coming to the therapeutic relationship and creating this particular type of intimacy does not involve exposing oneself as psychotherapist, neither does it mean to expose the other as client or patient. It rather means to come forward into this mutual space between us in which our common humanity is enhanced and where the client's problems and vulnerabilities can be safely considered by both of us. If I come to the relationship with a willingness to see what there is that you and I can learn about life through the experiences that you are struggling with, then neither I nor you will stand in the way of recognizing what is there for us to see. Instead of being overwhelmed by your experiences of stress and distress we can use the quiet process of dialogue to work our way through the experiences that you bring and we can begin to see their relevance to the way in which you live your life. The intimacy I create with you is about a daring to come to this place that we share, that we both know and that we can learn to shape and alter. If I do this I shall be moved and touched in my work with you and yet I shall not burden you with my own sorrows or desires.

It is Yeats, in his *Dialogue of Self and Soul*, who understood better than many a counsellor or psychotherapist what the objective of this encounter might be. The way in which he described it makes it clear that the work of patient dialoguing can lead to a new kind of contentment. We could do worse than following his lead and I would like to leave him the last word about dialogue and its desired outcome. It seems to me that the work of dialogue well accomplished throws light not only for the client but also for the counsellor or psychotherapist. In the work that happens in the therapeutic relationship we seek to find the source not only of the client's troubles but of human troubles in general, and therefore also of our own. If we devote ourselves to this search with our entire being and in the right spirit of forgiveness we may come somewhat closer to the source of life itself.

> I am content to follow to its source
> Every event in action or in thought
> Measure the lot; forgive myself the lot!
> When such as I cast out remorse
> So great a sweetness flows into the breast
> We must laugh and we must sing
> We are blest by everything
> Everything we look upon is blest.

(Yeats, 1950)

ALIENATION AND ADAPTATION: BEING A STRANGER IN A FOREIGN LAND

People are strange when you're a stranger,
Faces look ugly when you're alone.
Women seem wicked when you're unwanted
Streets are uneven when you are down.

(Jim Morrison, pop song of the 1960s)

We live in a world that favours travel. We live in a European Union where student exchanges are increasingly of the order of the day. We live in a transcultural world where young people of all nationalities and cultural origins come to live and study in each other's countries. We live in a world where many run the increasing risk of alienation and isolation.

Study or Work Abroad

It all sounds so good: to go and study or work abroad. The very idea of it conjures up an exciting and promising sense of adventure and enterprise. Travelling abroad seem like the epitome of human freedom. The reality is often very different and includes much loneliness, exclusion and culture shock. These things are hard to understand for those of us who are happily ensconced in the security of our home, our own country, our mother tongue and our family. As long as we travel for pleasure during our summer holidays, foreign countries just seem appealing and exotic. We envy those who get to spend a longer time abroad. Even when we see their obvious difficulties in integrating into the host culture we still tend to judge their problems as being fairly relative. We imagine that they will experience whatever they experience as a passing problem, as something temporary which is set in perspective against a background of a basic security about their origins and home base in their own country.

This may indeed be the case for people who come to stay in a new country for only a short while and who are accompanied by friends who speak their own language. They may taste the euphoria of the extended holiday, as their sense of belonging with their companions allows them to hold on to a clear point of reference in themselves and in relation to their roots.

Sometimes, of course, people do not fit well into their group and in that situation they may become more vulnerable to the impact of culture shock. They are in a similar situation to those people who migrate on their own initiative and by themselves. They often make a commitment for a longer time and try to integrate into the host country rather than remaining an observer and a visitor. Those who do so soon discover that you do not have to have a black skin in a white society in order to feel like an outcast.

On Your Own

It is easy to underestimate the importance of the societal structures that regulate belonging. As Sartre remarked, in his book *Anti-Semite and Jew* (Sartre, 1948):

> To own a hut in a village, it is not enough to have bought it with hard cash. One must know all the neighbours, their parents and grandparents, the surrounding farms, the beeches and oaks of the forest; one must know how to work, fish, hunt; one must have made notches in the trees of childhood and have found them enlarged in ripe old age.
>
> (Sartre, 1948, p. 83)

It is true that in order to feel one belongs in a society one has to partake in it and put down one's roots. As a foreigner you are by definition the intruder, who is only accepted as a temporary guest. You represent a particular interest to the people you meet and they take a very definite position in relation to you. You sense that they either relish or dislike this taste of difference that you give them. You always remain aware that you are related to in terms of the otherness that you carry in you. You know that you will always remain the outsider.

There is a sharp contrast between being this permanent stranger and being the temporary tourist. Being the stranger is to be alienated. It gives you that sinking feeling of no longer having any point of reference. To not belong anywhere leaves you stranded in no-man's land. To be without a home can give rise to the floundering and fluttering of insecurity or even to that of experiencing panic attacks. Freedom is one of the most scary things to handle and it consists of not being attached to anything. What we forget is that attachments are what secures us in the world and what gives things their meaning and context. Freedom is often used as a negative concept: what is attractive is the idea of being liberated from the ties that bind us. In reality the experience of absolute freedom is quite close to that of emptiness. Paradoxically, we cannot use our freedom when we have too much of it, for the more freedom there is the less certainty and less reality we have. As Colin Wilson once remarked, in his book *The Outsider*:

> The Outsider's sense of unreality cuts off his freedom at the root. It is as impossible to exercise freedom in an unreal world as it is to jump while you are falling.
>
> (Wilson, 1956, p. 49)

Foreign students often feel that the time of freedom that is available to them is marred by their lack of connectedness. They do not have enough of a foothold in reality to make the most of the open space they find themselves in as they crave some of the security they have left behind at home. Their insecurity is composed of many different elements that each may seem insignificant and small in their own right, but that together build a picture of disconnectedness and separateness which may seem unovercomable to some.

Physical Environment

The first basic factor that stops one feeling at home is simply not having a place of one's own. There is nowhere to call one's home: one lives in other people's spaces and smells and everything seems unsafe. The basic animal instinct for security is tampered with, a continuous state of alarm is set off. This experience is the more intense as one has fewer personal possessions to surround oneself with. Foreigners need objects to remind them of their home country and loved ones. I remember how attached I became to my old teddy-bear when I moved to France. To have a bit of safety suddenly becomes of stupendous importance. Other foreign students have shown me the special handkerchiefs (embroidered by grandmother) or the old sweater or pyjamas that they have become unexpectedly attached to all at once.

External Appearance

The experience of being unfamiliar with one's physical environment is often hard. To not be able to find one's direction and have no landmarks is very unsettling. Foreign students in a new, unknown city often have considerable trouble finding their way around and can report great distress over what would normally be a simple journey from A to B. A feeling of personal inadequacy is generated together with a physical sense of disorientation. This may be aggravated by the sense that one's body does not fit into the world as it used to. My excitement of being an 18-year-old foreign student in the South of France was muted into distress, as I felt treated like an object of curiosity by many of the French people I came into contact with. One of the hardest things was to discover how ill-matched I was to my surroundings, leaving me with a horrible sensation of being out of tune and out of step with everyone else. The French girls were small and delicate, and by comparison I felt gawky and far too tall. Most of the French boys were shorter than me as well and I used to feel like a giraffe standing in the queue at the restaurant universitaire. To tower over others is bad enough but to also be dressed differently and to have different-coloured eyes than everybody else can be an extremely alienating experience. My jeans were very much out of harmony with the little skirts and dresses around me and I did not really want to adjust to what seemed to me outmoded and unemancipated behaviour. But it made me feel terribly isolated to have to hold out for feminism all on my own. Foreign students from African countries have told me of their similar distress in deciding whether to adjust to a Western dress code. The conflict is between remaining dressed in the clothes that you used to feel comfortable in and that form a large part of your identity, or adjusting to your new environment and being more acceptable. On the one hand you may feel you betray your culture and value system if you accommodate, and on the other hand you may have to contend with feeling like the odd one out, behaving like an eccentric who attracts attention and who can easily become ridiculed. The irony of this is that clothes are the protective layer we wrap ourselves in so as to be safe and socially acceptable. When the clothes that used to be a source of comfort and strength instead become a source of discomfort and weakness, we definitely have a problem. We then have a choice between either adjusting our appearance in order to be accepted, or exposing and living out our difference boldly, courageously but often provocatively.

Social and Cultural Habits

This brings one to considering other social aspects of alienation in relation to the things that can no longer be indulged in freely and happily when living in another country. There is nothing grand or profound about this either. It is quite extraordinary to find that a large part of one's sense of security and identity is based on such simple things as the brand of butter or bread that one consumes. I remember indulging in French bread and croissants for three months at the beginning of my stay in France, only to get a terrible craving for good old Dutch brown bread. My German friend had similar frantic yearnings for German rye bread, but none of these things were at that time available in the south of France. We once had a special ceremony together, slowly consuming the bit of bread we had obtained from a friend who had come down to visit for a week: eating bread had suddenly been turned into a significant event. It was a good way of discovering things we had always taken for granted and learning to value the essentials of life.

Even more mundanely, we regularly complained to each other about the state the roads were in, remarking on how unsuited they were to our bicycles. We made quite a spectacle of ourselves riding around on those. Being together we felt superior to the French in this way and it allowed us to maintain our sense of importance, which otherwise would have been quickly eroded by having to make so very many efforts to fit in and being denied so many of what used to be essential habits. When my friend went back to Germany after one year and I was left by myself in France, things became a whole lot more difficult. Suddenly it was not so easy to continue riding a bike; it made me too self-conscious and too different to other people around me. I realized that in order to maintain myself I would have to learn to fit in and stop being so obviously different: I could no longer bear to be conspicuous on my own. My alliance to other foreigners had been eroded. My connections to my own past world had completely gone.

Language and Identity

At that moment the fact of my accent also became a real problem. It is terrible to know that one is recognizable as a stranger by the mere way in which one speaks. But of course the much more essential loss is that all the words one says have been altered and never quite have the same meaning as the meanings of one's childhood and one's group of reference. Language is the instrument through which we communicate with others and form bonds with them. The words we learn when we are young have special poignancy: they make us part of a social system that we adopt and that adopts us.

> Man is defined first of all as a being "in a situation". That means he forms a synthetic whole with his situation—biological, economic, political, cultural, etc. He cannot be distinguished from his situation, for it forms him and decides his possibilities.
>
> (Sartre, 1948, p. 60)

Language is what determines the strands with which we are attached to the world that moulds and nourishes us. When we give up our mother tongue for another language we are truly disabled and bereft. The initial struggle to acquire another language to a decent level of fluency is humiliating enough in itself. You find yourself babbling like a baby and unable to express the complex thoughts that used to flow from you so easily when you put them into what seemed like naturally available words. Now suddenly you have to rack your brain and the words still won't come and what is worse, other people judge your mental abilities by the sounds you make and that will not come at a greater speed than that of a four-year-old. You are truly diminished and deprived of your status of adult and no longer accepted fully.

As soon as you stop believing in your own ability to communicate you will have a tendency to flee from others and hide away on your own or find others who understand and speak your mother tongue. If you come from a small minority culture this may not be possible. I have never been able to hide away in speaking Dutch when I was in France and have only rarely met people to speak Dutch with in England. To never hear one's mother tongue spoken, not in the street, not on the radio or on television, is a terribly lonely business that makes you feel as if you belong to a strange sect or subset of the population, for which there is not really any room.

The more subtle fact of not being able to swear with the words that keep coming naturally in your mother tongue, or to have to fall back on your own language when doing mental arithmetic because the times tables are stuck in your brain in one language only, adds to a sense of never being able to fully integrate. With different languages also come different ways of expressing yourself. The tone of different languages and their emphasis on certain concepts makes for a very different way of experiencing yourself. If you are ever to become part of your new culture, you know you have to lend yourself to such a deep transformation as well.

I learnt that I had to let myself get much more passionate if I ever wanted to speak French well, and then of course I had to learn to get much more phlegmatic and rational when trying to get my English right: each time bringing out different aspects of my character, leaving the Dutch pragmatism somewhat behind. Not everyone is willing and able to make such adjustments and no-one ever makes them fully and completely. If one experiences the demands of the host culture as an imposition it can become quite a nightmare to live in it for any stretch of time. A young Arab student once told me that she could not cope with the way in which British culture was angular and mathematically organized: she missed the fluency and roundness of the architecture, culture and language and music back home and had a physical abhorrence of lots of things that just seemed too Western, dull and square, lacking in elegance, shape and colour. She often felt physically sick at this dissonance in her world. It is hardly surprising that the incidence of emotional problems is so very much higher for foreigners than for natives, in any country in the world. As soon as you uproot yourself you make yourself vulnerable: you go out on a limb. Even Freud experienced great problems of insecurity when he went as a student to work with Charcot in Paris. In his correspondence with his fianceé Martha he reports how it led him to become reliant on cocaine! (Jones, 1953).

Being an Outsider by Vocation

There are four potential solutions to the predicaments described in this chapter. The first is to go back home and make the most of having travelled and of having been away and having learnt to appreciate and embrace the comforts of one' s home. The second is to stay abroad and to become integrated with the local population as much as possible. This always remains problematic because in one's heart one continues to be other. The third solution is to remain abroad but to stay with a community of people from one's home country: this is the solution of many immigrants who build a home from home and hang on to their original identity. This may work for the first generation but evokes considerable problems for the next generations, who have to stand in the tension between two cultures on a permanent basis. The final and fourth solution is to become integrated to a whole new class of rootless, international people, to become as it were identified with the idea of not belonging. After having lived abroad for long enough this is often the only solution as one becomes aware that one does no longer belong either in one's country of origin nor ever completely in the host country.

It is a difficult thing to accept that one speaks with an accent everywhere one goes and that people in every country will continue to enquire how long one has been here or is here for. It makes one feel very low and often unwelcome. The solution is to adopt this new identity of belonging to the international class: the adaptive set, the travelling elite, the ones who know what it feels like to be outcast.

What Sartre said about the Jews applies here:

Jewish authenticity consists in choosing oneself as Jew—that is , in realizing one's Jewish condition. The authentic Jew abandons the myth of the universal man; he knows himself and wills himself into history as a historic and damned creature; he ceases to run away from himself and to be ashamed of his own kind. He understands that society is bad; for the naive monism of the inauthentic Jew he substitutes a social pluralism. He knows that he is one who stands apart, untouchable, scorned, proscribed—and it is as such that he asserts his being.

(Sartre, 1948, p. 111)

In other words, when one feels outcast and isolated the best way forward is to accept one's status and stop fighting for integration. To integrate into a new status quo is to become again like an object—to opt again for immutability and become set in stone. The best source of a new identity is not to hold on to one's origins, but to embrace the new position of foreigner wholeheartedly. To take such a position and such an attitude to one's predicament opens a new dimension of integration. The choice is no longer between adjusting to one culture or staying true to another but rather to overcoming both by creating a new identity of the person who never fully belongs. Incredible support and loyalty can exist between people from different cultural backgrounds who have been united by the same predicament of feeling exiled. And the creation of this new nationality of stateless people could hold much promise in solving problems for future generations. For the melting pot that we now live in will continue to shake our cultures and populations together and will require of us a new flexibility and an ability to let go of previous securities in belonging to a country or culture. Travellers are the active agents of change in society and their role will become increasingly important. There are intense dangers in nationalism and the need to assert national identification—we cannot afford to be so ensconced.

The Challenge and Value of Migration

Those who let themselves be challenged by the trials and tribulations of foreign travel, work and study may well be the embodiment of the new values that we need for a multi-cultural future. These are values that no longer set out to protect vested interests and instead seek to establish what is feasible in a world where certainties are constantly challenged. Through migrating and finding one's usual assumptions undermined and contradicted one discovers new sides to the same old questions. This enables one to not take sides, but to view things from a variety of positions and to relativize one's own opinions, mitigating them with new input. Such flexibility of perspective is an essential asset for life in the world of tomorrow, where people from different nations will have to get on with each other in ever-closer co-operation in a shrinking world.

For those of us who do not find ourselves in a position to experience this process of experimentation with foreignness, there is some hope in other forms. For we can be travellers and foreigners in many different ways, between classes and social systems, cities and neighbourhoods and cultures of lots of different sorts. Thus, we can all find out a little about what it means to feel contradicted, unaccepted, alien and scorned. It is on this internal knowledge of our own estrangement that we should draw when working with strangers. From them we can learn much about our own prejudices and pet hatreds and we can continue our own education second-hand in this way. If we are privileged enough to work with many different nationalities, a new picture eventually emerges. We no longer see only difference and variety, but we begin to see the underlying similarities. We begin to recognize the fundamental human issues that all cultures and nationalities are concerned with. We can begin to tell the difference between what is a basic human need and what is a secondary cultural habit. At this point we become less obsessed with cultural relativism and can work with the alienation people feel, no matter what its origin.

Then we are in a position to really work with people instead of seeing the foreigner. We can play a small role in the integration of nations and ease some of the tensions for those who do not fit in and do not feel they can ever belong. In some ways all forms of counselling and psycho-therapy are about this: those who come to us are always alienated and although not always foreign by culture, they often feel foreign by nature. And all these strangers and alienated people need someone to under-stand them and translate what they are saying. In adopting an attitude of openness to the confusion that such work may confront us with, we can improve our work and we can become better strangers to each other and thus better known to each other and ourselves. The objective is not to soothe the other's anxieties and make the other welcome and feel they belong—but rather to help them be strong in the midst of insecurity and find a new dignity in coping with the dialectic of their difference.

Conclusion

In final analysis it helps to keep in mind that when faced with alienation one is likely to go through several phases. The first is to hark back to the past and to one's previous identity. The second is to wallow in the sorrow of being an alien and an outcast. The third is to try and adapt anxiously to the new culture and assume a false identity. The fourth is to use the opportunity of being challenged to the core and let oneself flounder into uncertainty. It is only when discovering one's ability to survive in the midst of doubt that a new identity can be shaped. This consists of having confidence in one's ultimate flexibility.

3

PASSION

A PASSION FOR LIFE: REDISCOVERING THE INTENSITY OF LIVING

The heart has its reasons which reason knows nothing of.
(Blaise Pascal, *Pensées*, 1662)

The ruling passion, be it what it will, the ruling passion conquers reason still.
(Alexander Pope, *Moral Essays*; see Pope, 1963)

The dictionary these days defines "passion" as no more than strong emotion. Yet the word passion comes from the Latin verb *patior*, which means to suffer, to tolerate, to endure. Passion, etymologically speaking, refers to the passive experience of being exposed to the dramas of life that cause us to suffer. Passion in this sense refers to our response to a world that holds much challenge and misfortune, all of which we have to accept and take in our stride. Passionate engagement with life is the opposite of determined voluntarism. It has a quality of fatefulness and inexorability. In passion we are overwhelmed and out of control. We do not manoeuvre and manipulate ourselves into passion, we rather find ourselves moved and drawn into it.

Limit Situations

To be passionate about life is to let ourselves be dictated to by fate. It means to let ourselves be summoned and called into question. To be passionate is to be prepared to go to the limit and to discover and surrender to laws greater than ourselves. In passion we give of ourselves without reserve and stretch ourselves beyond our previous boundaries, into the unknown. In doing so we eventually come up against a natural limit. Karl Jaspers described very clearly how life has a way of bringing us up against such limit situations sooner or later. He said:

In our day-to-day lives we often evade them, by closing our eyes and living as if they did not exist. We forget that we must die, forget our guilt, and forget that we are at the mercy of chance.

(Jaspers, 1951, p. 20)

Most of us live passionless lives for much of the time, because it is easier and more reassuring. We can pretend to stay in control as long as we manage to steer clear of limit situations. We tread carefully. We live cautiously. We hold our breath. We play it safe. We constrict ourselves voluntarily and stop life flowing through our veins. For this relative safety we pay the price of a decreasing sense of vitality until we flounder into futility and boredom.

A Sense of Failure

We might even forget that we have the option of exposing ourselves to the ups and downs of more intense experiences at any time. When we are tempted to open ourselves to a sense of elation or destiny we often slow ourselves down for fear of the consequences. We know from experience that openness and passion will bring disappointments and suffering as well. So we rein ourselves in. Jaspers said:

The ultimate situations—death, chance, guilt and the uncertainty of the world—confront me with the reality of failure. What do I do in the face of this absolute failure, which if I am honest I cannot fail to recognise?

(Jaspers, 1951, p. 22)

We can be so anxious to avoid such reminders of mortality and failure that we studiously eliminate any hint of drama and intensity, discarding passion from our lives. As counsellors and therapists we often content ourselves with the vicarious experiences of the passionate adventures of our clients. We stand by passively as they take the risks and suffer through human tragedies and dramas. We look upon our clients' difficulties with a weary eye and, whilst we might be entranced by some of their experiences, we do our best to bring them back to something more sensible, more modest and more mediocre, in other words something a little more like our own lives.

At the same time, we can sometimes get quite bored listening to clients who have made avoidance the central credo of their lives. We want them to experience something new and revitalizing and we know instinctively that it would do them a world of good to be challenged by life and suffer a little instead of avoiding and shirking and hiding away from life.

An Essential Ingredient of Life

Pascal already understood how important it is to have a modicum of passion in one's life and to not let oneself be robbed of it by trying to eliminate risk. He gave the example of the passion for gambling:

> A given man lives a life free from boredom by gambling a small sum every day. Give him every morning the money he might win that day, but on condition that he does not gamble, and you will make him unhappy. It might be argued that what he wants is the entertainment of gaming and not the winnings. Make him play then for nothing; his interest will not be fired and he will become bored, so it is not just entertainment he wants. A half-hearted entertainment without excitement will bore him. He must have excitement, he must delude himself into imagining that he would be happy to win what he would not want as a gift if it meant giving up gambling. He must create some target for his passions and then arouse his desire, anger, fear, for this object he has created, just like children taking fright at a face they have daubed themselves.
>
> (Pascal (1662), *Pensées* No. 136, p. 70)

We need our passions and we value them greatly, even though they trouble us and make life a great deal more difficult for us. It seems as if life, when confronted head on, is essentially about chaos, trials and tribulations. Life is difficult and complicated: it demands complete commitment. Death, by contrast, is easy and straightforward. Dead things can be organized: death brings peace and is achieved by surrender. Surrendering to passion, then, is like inviting death into the middle of life. To yield to passion is to find temporary peace, but this momentary death in the middle of life precisely confronts us with the contradictions and paradoxes that we had tried to avoid before.

Desire and Reason

Now we have to take account of both our longings and the eventual impossibility of their fulfilment. We have to learn to be valiant in the battle between our desires and our reason. Although we often believe that reason is the most important human asset and that we should learn to let rationality set the tone of our lives, reason is usually secondary to passion. As David Hume pointed out:

> We speak not strictly and philosophically when we talk of the combat of passion and of reason. Reason is, and ought only to be, the slave of the passions, and can never pretend to any other office than to serve and obey them.
>
> (Hume, 1739, p. 415)

Reason is the unifying force of intelligence with which we try to hold together and make sense of what the passions reveal to us in all their contradictions and complexity. Reason organizes and makes safe what is originally confused and dangerous and which appeals to us through the senses.

When we work with people on the problems and predicaments that they are struggling with in their lives, we start from their sensations, their experiences and their passions and then we try to put some order and understanding into all of that. Some therapeutic approaches favour the free expression of the emotions, in the belief that cathartic experience will clear the air and give relief. Such approaches usually fall within the humanistic tradition. Other approaches favour rational solutions, aiming to minimize passion and maximize reason until choices can be made that are sensible, assuming these will lead to the best possible outcome. These approaches are broadly speaking within the cognitive-behavioural tradition. Other approaches try to understand the reasons behind the emotional experiences, encouraging a continuous process of self-reflectiveness which is supposed to sort the difficulties out. These are known as the psychodynamic and psychoanalytic approaches.

Forerunners of Psychotherapy of the Passions

Interestingly, these various brands of psychotherapeutic interventions correspond to ancient philosophical traditions of 2000 years ago. Hellenistic philosophy shows the whole range of these diverse views of human nature and proposes concrete ways to attain the objective of conducting a well-lived life. According to these different schools of thought, eudaimonia, or the flourishing life, could be achieved in a number of ways (Nussbaum, 1994).

Plato insisted on the principle of virtue, which was supposed to overcome any contradictory emotions. He alleged that it was possible to reason through any difficulties and approach life with a rational and calm, philosophical attitude, that would cut through the emotions and leave us in control. Aristotle had a slightly less idealistic approach, as he taught people to sift through their opinions, separating true and false beliefs and adjusting their emotions accordingly. For Aristotle it was more important to be realistic and let oneself be immersed in the world and then learn to manage the emotions this brought about, whereas for Plato the objective was to make the emotions unnecessary by putting order into life in relation to an ideal.

The Epicureans had yet another way of dealing with emotional predicaments, which was to cultivate detachment and just not let the problems of the world matter too much. The Epicurean view was that pleasure is the only good and that we should learn to maximize pleasure, cultivating its natural sources and eliminate pain by discarding all false beliefs. The Sceptics took this idea of detachment even further by suggesting the possibility of eliminating pain by eliminating all beliefs, not just the false ones. The Stoics transformed this notion by suggesting that it was possible to educate and alter one's soul by the use of logic and poetry, so that through self-control one could achieve ultimate value and virtue.

It is interesting to note that all of these classical philosophies are based on the premise of having to restrict the human passions. This is something that is shared by most psychotherapies. Yet getting rid of passion as do the Sceptics, minimizing it as do the Epicureans, or increasing control over it as do the Stoics, are no ultimate solutions if we want to live a life that is full and vibrant.

Constriction or Expansion?

To help other people understand themselves or to assist them in setting right what is wrong with their lives may not be best done by restricting their experience. It may not be constriction but expansion that is required. As argued before, in our culture the problem is not that people have too much on their plates, but rather not enough. They live futile and constricted lives. They live in a vacuum of meaning, as Frankl (1946) remarked.

Humanistic psychology rediscovered passion in the 1960s and encouraged people to get in touch with their experience in a fuller sense. Some of the therapies that were developed as part of the human potential movement strove to give people full access to their emotionality in a rather simplistic fashion. Out of these early stirrings of passion the counselling movement grew. This rapidly developed into a skills-based technology, which replaced the original enthusiasms with a more rational approach. Counselling has become so sensible that it often restricts itself to what can be carefully overseen and packaged into a neat formulation of good practice. The bulk of professional work these days is kept to careful boundaries and proceeds in an orderly fashion, making measured and responsible interventions keeping clients' experience within the bounds of the acceptable.

Yet, human nature is such that it does not really thrive on such ordered interventions. The significant transformations of life are made at moments that may seem chaotic and that are experienced as extraordinary. They require the personal and the unexpected: they require the tools and properties of passion.

Clients' Experiences of Passion

This brings up the question of the extent to which we can afford to engross ourselves in our clients' real longings and yearnings, their genuine concerns, their true aspirations and their most deeply felt passions. This is not so much a matter of skill or technique or empathy as a matter of resonance and co-presence. I cannot teach myself to understand another person's heartfelt concerns. I can only recognize an other's preoccupations if I have experienced similar ones for myself. I can only tune into the level of concern that I have been capable of descending or rising to in myself (van Deurzen-Smith, 1995).

In the final analysis, as a counsellor or psychotherapist I am only as competent with my clients as I have been with myself. I am the measure of my capacity for passion and I can only ally myself with the suffering and yearning of my clients to the extent that I have gone through the fire of such challenges myself. I can, of course, accompany many people on journeys that lead to familiar places, but I can only take a person safely through to a new phase of his or her life if I have a personal acquaintance with the intensity that such passionate new involvement will require of him or her.

There are many clients who come for counselling or therapy when they are on the verge of a breakthrough in their lives. This elicits a lot of anxiety. The anxiety can be seen as the readiness for adventure, the gearing up for the special intensity that is required to embark on this new part of their life. But it can only be experienced in such a positive fashion if there is enough confidence and trust that the venture is manageable and will lead to something valuable. Otherwise the anxiety will be a tense and fearful experience that clients will avoid and evade as best they can. If they cannot avoid the anxiety, but cannot manage it either, it may plunge them into a frantic state of mind that leads to breakdown rather than breakthrough.

Passionate living is anxious living: it leads to energy levels beyond what is usual and normally acceptable. To care deeply about a new thing or person in one's life and to want something with all one's might is a terrifying experience that exposes us to new possibilities of loss and to the likelihood of having to admit defeat at some point. If we do not have a basic belief in the rightness of taking such risks, of the value of living life to the full, then the rise of anxiety can lead to panic rather than to passion. It can block our progress rather than facilitate and enhance it. Good psychotherapists and counsellors understand such predicaments and they find ways of letting the new energy flow in a constructive direction, encouraging the generation of passion rather than panic, whilst carefully monitoring the realism of the enterprise and the possibility of consequences beyond what was bargained for.

It requires a lot of the counsellor or the therapist to stand in the real tensions of life with clients in this manner. It is much easier to observe clients at a distance and calm their passions down by artful interpretations and rational considerations. As our own lives are managed more tightly we will be inclined to be more cautious about our clients' passions as well. When we are able to let ourselves be opened up by life again, our interventions in clients' lives will be altered automatically and we shall provide an entirely new kind of enthusiasm and trust in the process of life.

Laura's Experience

Two years ago I worked with a client who was having a torrid affair with a married man and who was much perturbed by the impact this had on her life. Laura, as I called her when I wrote up my work with her (van Deurzen-Smith, 1997), was in need of some help in understanding and balancing her own reactions to this man. She was, however, completely unready to give up her passion, which had woken her up and had made her alive in a way she had not known before. She rightly valued this relationship beyond even her own peace of mind, and in some ways it cut across her ability to think clearly in moral terms. She had lost track, for instance, of her responsibility in relation to her lover's children, whom she did not want to think about at all. I was inclined to take a rather superior stance to her predicament, as I was inwardly condemning her for her waywardness and immorality. I was, at that time, myself married, having been in a mutually faithful relationship for 17 years. I naturally assumed that my own state of relative calm and contentment was the norm against which I should observe Laura. If I am honest with myself, I considered my own state to be the better one to which I would like to see my client aspire. At the same time, I experienced a sense of resonance with her predicament and in particular with her longing for intensity and challenge in the relationship. I had the uneasy feeling that she might be attuned to something important that I had long lost sight of for myself.

I focused many of my interventions on helping her to be more sensible in her evaluation of her own experience. I wanted to "cure" her of this intense and, I thought, rather destructive love. I did not impose these judgements on her, but I held them nevertheless and I had to struggle with what she and I both experienced as a rather condemning streak that made me try to get her to toe the line of moral convention rather more than she wanted to at this point in her life. I have never believed in merely backing people in doing what they want to be doing. I consider it to be enormously important that people weigh up the effects of their actions and that they think of the consequences of their passions and longings. I do not believe that we can make judgements about what is right and wrong, but we can have some sense of what effects might be beneficial or harmful and what we want or are able to live with in the long run. Values are an important guideline to our choices and decisions and clients have to learn to pitch their passions to the things that they passionately want in the long run.

Looking at It the Other Way Around

Before they can do this they need to first have passions to help them find out what it is they desperately want. We need to help our clients pinpoint the stirrings of passion and to help them express the emotions that lead to it; only then can we understand what values they point to. As the philosopher Collingwood pointed out:

> Until a man has expressed his emotion, he does not yet know what emotion it is. The act of expressing it is therefore an exploration of his own emotions. He is trying to find out what these emotions are.
> (Collingwood, 1958, *The Principles of Art*, p. 111)

What we have to assume is that passions, in principle, are good and make sense. We allow them free rein until they speak loudly and clearly and a new perspective on the world emerges. Then we have to check whether the things that we want are really worthwhile and realistic and whether they lead to some feasible future. To oversee the consequences of one's passions is an important counterpart to letting them develop.

In all this we must remember that what is right for one person is not necessarily right for another. Having assessed my own mistakes in my work with Laura, and having been through some personal and passionate challenges of my own, when I worked a little later with a client whom I called Rosa (see Chapter 2) I was able to take a very different line. With Rosa I realized that her experience of an unhappy love was deeply valid and valuable to her. It made her capable of absorbing new strength into herself and she did not want to be cured of this suffering in her life. I was capable of standing by her and allowing her to learn to bear her pain and see the positive challenges in her experience of passion. Even though it brought her much pain, it brought her a much greater aliveness and strength as well.

Not All the Same

Some of us are more adept at living with passion than others. Some people's talents are more suited to living a quiet, peaceful, regulated life and other people's temperaments require a life of intense passion and challenge. We should not take ourselves as the measure of these things but allow each of our clients to find the right level of tension and passion for themselves. George Eliot once observed how some people just need to be stretched and how yearning may turn into martyrdom, if that is the only manner in which passion seems to be available. She described the life of St Theresa, saying:

> Theresa's passionate, ideal nature demanded an epic life: what were many-volumed romances of chivalry and the social conquests of a brilliant girl to her? Her flame quickly burned up that light fuel; and fed from within, soared after some illimitable satisfaction, some object which would never justify weariness, which would reconcile self-despair with the rapturous consciousness of life beyond self. She found her epos in the reform of a religious order.
>
> (Eliot, 1872)

It is clear that some people crave space so that their spirit may soar. They want to learn to spread their wings and fly and discover new landscapes over the horizon. Others find it difficult to even find the beginning of courage and an appetite for adventure and passion. They hide from life and hope they can avoid being stretched even by inevitable brushes with fate and destiny.

Psychotherapists and counsellors have to make distinctions between people who need to calm their passions to manageable proportions, people who need to be supported in going for what their heart pulls them towards, and people who need to learn to listen a little more to the contradictions they are struggling with. We can only do these things for our clients to the extent that we have let some light into ourselves. We do not have to live through Greek tragedies, but we must at least be able to resonate moderately with the call of the night and the passion for life.

We need to learn to say "yes" to life and to be attentive to what lies hidden underneath everyday things. If we let ourselves be moved by life and become at least capable of passion again, we shall be confronted with our limitations and the sorrows of life as well as its pleasures. It is to not be afraid of that mix of reality that secures a life of toughness and light, making the world meaningful and worthwhile. We need, in other words, to dare to face the human condition.

Camus spoke of Sisyphus as the epitome of the human condition. Sisyphus, having offended the Gods, is punished by having to roll a stone up a hill and see it roll down again over and over again without any hope of respite or redemption. His life seems absurd. Yet he concludes that even that absurd life can evoke human passion and that living it fully can fill a human heart. Sisyphus can be passionate as well as patient, he can be joyful as well as tragic:

> His fate belongs to him. His rock is his thing. Likewise, the absurd man, when he contemplates his torment, silences all the idols. In the universe suddenly restored to its silence, the myriad wondering little voices of the earth rise up. Unconscious, secret calls, invitations from all the faces, they are the necessary reverse and price of victory. There is no sun without shadow, and it is essential to know the night. The absurd man says yes and his effort will henceforth be unceasing.
>
> (Camus, 1942, p. 98).

Conclusion

To have a passion for life means to embrace life in all its contradictions and to not be too afraid to be devastated and hurt. It means to take a risk and let oneself flounder, discovering the true contrasts of the paradoxes of life and death, of day and night. As Paul Tillich pointed out:

> A life process is the more powerful, the more non-being it can include in its self-affirmation, without being destroyed by it. The neurotic can include only a little non-being, the average man a limited amount, the creative man a large amount, God— symbolically speaking—an infinite amount. The self-affirmation of a being in spite of non-being is the expression of its power of being.
>
> (Tillich, 1954, p. 40)

In the process of letting life matter again passionately, we rediscover our creativity. In the chaos of life and in the throes of our passion we learn to be whole, to be both wrong and right.

IF TRUTH WERE A WOMAN: REALITY AND MEANING

In Search of Truth

Nietzsche wrote in his book, *Beyond Good and Evil*:

> Suppose truth is a woman—what then? . . . What is certain is that she has not allowed herself to be won—and today every kind of dogmatism is left standing distressed and discouraged.
>
> (Nietzsche, 1886)

It is more than a century ago that Nietzsche made this claim that science and philosophy were bankrupt and impotent in relation to the truths that they pursued but never grasped. Today our sciences have brought even more information and technology. We control and manipulate our environment in new and sophisticated ways. We can protect ourselves from many threats and we have achieved relatively secure access to the resources that keep us fed and watered, clean and warm. Our physical workload is performed largely by machines. At least some of us are comfortable and we continue our constant progress towards more comfort and ease. The natural sciences are the source of the industrial and technological civilization on which Western society has pinned its hopes for survival and growth.

The Limitations of Science and Technology

In the past few decades it has, however, begun to dawn on us that unlimited growth and expansion may be a recipe for extinction instead of survival. What we call "progress" often creates as many problems as it cures. The cars that transport people with speed can also kill them and their exhaust fumes toxify the environment. The nuclear energy that was harnessed to benefit civilization is capable of destroying human life on the planet. The undisciplined use of natural resources for the benefit of some leads to the exploitation of others and erodes the land that provides for us.

It is therefore relevant to question whether our sciences have brought us enlightenment as well as knowledge and wisdom as well as control. The same question can also be addressed to the social sciences which, in their attempt to insert the human being into their investigation of the world, often alienate us from our experience instead of bringing it home to us for better scrutiny. As Western culture becomes increasingly fragmented, superficial and impermanent, some have begun to wonder if science does not rob us of as many things as it has brought us. When we stop rushing along with the mad pace of the end of the millennium towards the next experiment, the next set of statistics, the next achievement, the next expansion, we find ourselves confronted with a vacuum of meaning. We may know the facts but the values elude us. We may have successfully focused on the detail, but in the process the global picture has become unclear. We have become short-sighted.

Fact and Fiction

Perhaps we should not be surprised that this is so for, as T.S. Eliot put it so succinctly, it seems that:

> Human kind cannot bear very much reality.
>
> (Eliot, 1994b, "Burnt Norton")

The more we know, the less we seem able to think about the purpose and meaning of it all. We are a bit like those prisoners in Plato's cave (Plato, 1955) who spent their time staring at the wall of their prison, where they could see the shadows of the real world. They were so used to being in chains and guessing at the meaning of the external events reflected on the wall of the cave that they were loath to be unchained and taken out into the open to see the world with their own eyes. Some of them were so absorbed in the abstract study of shadows that they were unable to conceive of the existence of a real world at all. They were so used to their blinkers and darkness that to be faced with the light would have blinded them. In many respects this simile has become more relevant with the passing of two millennia.

Heidegger, in his 1951 lecture entitled *What is called thinking?* (1954), said:

> Most thought-provoking in our thought-provoking time is that we are still not thinking.
>
> (Heidegger, 1954, p. 6)

By "thinking" Heidegger did not mean the rational thought with which we calculate and control the world, but the process of deep reflection and meditation through which we open ourselves to being. Doing so produces wonder about life and death and all that is, in a way that is inconceivable when we merely manipulate the world. Thinking takes us out of the virtual reality that human beings have created and brings us back in touch with underlying or overarching truths. This is, of course, rather different to Freud's peeling of the onion and the subsequent psychoanalytic delving into the unconscious, which is an intrapsychic journey rather than an ontological one.

A Margin of Freedom

Freud argued that human beings need to develop the psychic structure of the ego to mediate between themselves and the world. Heidegger argued that we mediate between ourselves and the world through the meanings that we create about the world, others and ourselves. One thing that Freud and Heidegger do agree on is that what we usually think of as reality is nothing but its surface and that it is essential to look a little further if we want to understand the wider truths of human living.

When we do so we notice that human beings, in spite of their extensive achievements in exploring the surface level of reality, tend to hide away from such deeper truths. This is undoubtedly related to the fact that we tackle the world through the mediation of tools, clothes, houses, language and theories. There is always some amount of distance between ourselves and the world and therefore some measure of freedom in how we approach it. As Sartre (1943a) observed, human beings are not condemned to act out any specific role in the world. They can invent and reinvent themselves and indeed have to create themselves in order to become anything at all. It is through our actions that we become what we are and in the process we give meaning to the world.

> In this world where I engage myself, my acts cause values to spring up like partridges.
>
> (Sartre, 1943a, p. 38)

Whilst Sartre may have somewhat overestimated the number of options open to us, his work was a potent reminder of our margin of freedom. He also urgently drew attention to the responsibilities that this involves. We are flexible and adaptable and capable of imagining and creating as well as perceiving and receiving.

Children's process of growing up is not just about physical maturation or social adaptation, it is also about learning to tell stories about the world that make this world meaningful to them. This human ability to create meaning goes well beyond that of simple assimilation of and accommodation to what is there. It extends to the capacity for making up, inventing or distorting reality. Children learn to come to grips with the world as they find it by telling and acting out stories, by making paintings and by creating worlds of make-believe. In this process they discover their ability to alter reality and to create meanings of their own that do not coincide with the facts. In other words, they learn to lie.

Learning to Lie

It is essential for every child to explore the limits of human inventiveness and freedom in this way. First, the child discovers how to distort, magnify or diminish reality. Then it discovers about concealing truth and lying. It is a crucial moment of human development when a child is caught lying and is corrected. It is reassuring to find that one cannot take endless liberties with the truth and that there really is a shared reality that matters and that keeps us together. People can only discover what truth is by coming up against its limits. We cannot discover about truth without coming to terms with untruth and we cannot know about right until we know about wrong.

I remember the day that I discovered about the consequences of lying. It happened at the age of six or seven, when, playing with a gang of friends in the Dutch dunes, I tore a perfectly good skirt climbing over a barbed wire fence. The older children in the gang told me to stay quiet about this, as I would otherwise expose our illicit tramping into no-go areas which would lead to punishment for all. First I tried to hide the skirt, under my pillow. My mother found it almost immediately. Then I tried to pretend that I thought there was nothing wrong with the skirt. This was a vain evasion as I had already made it clear that there was something wrong by hiding the skirt. When my mother stood pointing at the damage, interrogating me about its origin, I shamefully told her that my skirt had caught on a branch of a tree. She wanted to know where I had been climbing trees.

I now had to weave a whole web of lies because there were no climbing trees in the area where we had been playing. I felt forced to say that we had been to the woods instead. This made my mother rather upset. The woods were forbidden territory, because there had been a case of child abduction there. My lying seemed to be getting me into worse trouble than the truth would have warranted. By now I felt utterly miserable about this deceit. My mother smelled a rat. She expertly questioned and coaxed me, until eventually I confessed the story to her, because I could no longer accommodate my duplicity. There were no consequences other than a mild reminder not to trespass and not to lie. The sheer sense of relief at being able to level with her again and to know that she would trust me in return was immense. I never forgot that lesson and realized that it was important to strive to be open and truthful if one wants to be close to a person. It also taught me that there is a bottom line of truth that cannot be denied. Such truth is based in factual and shared reality.

The Price of Deceit

I am now more certain than ever that constructive human relations are only possible within a framework of commitment to truth. I believe that it is shared truth that defines and safeguards relationship. The extent to which I am open with someone and am able to participate in the same broad framework of meaning and reality defines the level of our mutuality, trust and togetherness. This is why couples inevitably pay the high price of fragmentation and alienation when they betray mutual trust. In this sense it could be said that truth is human rather than woman, for truth is the essential ingredient of human relating and where it is shared and valued it melds people together into larger units. Where truth is not shared it pushes people apart.

My daughter Sasha, when she was eight, took this discovery a step further. She confessed to me, walking up to school one day, that she had said to her friends that she is the one who always gets told off at home when she and her brother have a row. She knew this to be an untruth, as it was an old bone of contention in the family that it was Benjamin, the eldest by five years, who tended to bear the brunt of our dissatisfaction when the children were fighting. We generally maintained that he should take more responsibility than his younger sister as he was older, wiser, stronger and a whole lot taller and heavier. He argued convincingly that this was often unfair as she could be just as wily as him, if not more so, and get him into lots of trouble.

My daughter telling her friends that she was the one singled out for our criticism was a misrepresentation of the truth, as she herself acknowledged. She said to me that it made her feel bad to have said this, because when the other children found out the truth, as she assumed they inevitably would, they would not believe in her anymore. This, she said, would make her lonely. But as we discussed the situation further she found that the very fact of her having to hide the truth from her friends was already making her lonely: either way, lying had isolated her from them and had generated discomfort in her. This was an important discovery for her. It encouraged her to be frank with her friends but it also made her much more willing to openly consider the ins and outs of her relationship to her brother.

Her distortion of the truth demonstrated her desire to be seen as capable of bearing responsibility in conflict. She was, as it were, play-acting at being so grown-up that she would, like her brother, be held responsible for her behaviour. This brought home to her that being accountable for her part in what goes on between herself and others is a sign of strength and something to aspire to. Her experience demonstrated that she had reached the stage where she could stop being either victimized or spared, two sides of the same coin. The whole episode was about her mastering a new ability to be in charge of her actions and their consequences. Facing the truth of discomfort about not being truthful opened up all of that and more. It takes considerable courage to accept the consequences in this way. Most of us would rather continue to tell ourselves fine stories about our situation in the world that let us off the hook. Learning to be truthful at the age of eight is no guarantee that we can face all the other truths about ourselves, others and the world we live in that we continue to discover for the rest of our lives. Sometimes we need to go to a psychotherapist or a counsellor to be helped in confronting truth and finding meaning again.

Truth and Psychotherapy

Many clients initially come to psychotherapy not to discover and confront truth but to establish that they are right. They do this either by trying to get the psychotherapist to empathize and agree with them, or by fighting the therapist and proving him or her wrong. This puts a special strain on the therapeutic relationship and requires the psychotherapist or counsellor to be able to provide a steady presence and function as a reliable point of reference. On the one hand, the psychotherapist has to be able to resonate empathetically with the subjective experience of the client. On the other hand, the psychotherapist has to be able to keep hold of a wider perspective on truth.

This raises the tricky question of what the truth of human living really is and how it relates to our clients' predicaments. The issue of truth is a sore point in the profession and it is usually diplomatically avoided because it is too controversial. It seems to me that avoiding this question is irresponsible in the extreme. Psychotherapy and counselling professionals behave a bit like their clients: avoiding facing the core issues and hiding their heads in the sand of their everyday practices instead.

The fact is that the many different approaches to psychotherapy and counselling that have been developed over the past century have very different views of truth. These views are implicit in what psychotherapists and counsellors do, but they are rarely made explicit.

Cognitive and Behavioural Version of Truth

Cognitive and behavioural approaches to psychotherapy and counselling are concerned with that which is socially and culturally desirable and acceptable. They aim to help the person to readjust to the norm of rational and adaptive behaviour and they see their role in terms of correcting faulty thinking and acting. This makes these approaches relatively easy to evaluate as their measure of "truth" can be standardized. You know when a person has been able to perform a particular social task, so you can measure whether the therapeutic intervention has effectively enabled him or her to do so. It begs the question, however, of whether this fitting in to the social norm is desirable and whether it defines truth about human well-being. Just because you can hold down a job does not mean that you have made sense of the feeling of anxiety that made you ill at ease with your work. If you have not made sense of it but have been merely taught to suppress it, you may well have lost an opportunity to take stock of your life and take a new, more satisfactory direction and avoiding future disenchantment.

Psychoanalytic and Psychodynamic Version of Truth

Psychoanalytic and psychodynamic approaches tend to define truth in a much more relative manner. They emphasize the internal operation of the individual psyche and have designed a number of concepts that make it possible to explain subjective experience in theoretical and often causal terms. This makes it much more difficult to do outcome studies, as the goal is not primarily to cure or adjust, but rather to explain a person's reality. By naming internal processes and understanding them in dynamic terms, new meanings emerge. This may in turn improve the person's ability to cope with life, although it can equally encourage a kind of self-absorption that is not necessarily conducive to positive social outcomes. Research done in this field is mainly descriptive in nature, rather than quantitative. According to many theorists, psychoanalytic truths are narrative and not historical in nature. They are contingent on time and place and can only attain a pragmatic and local or regional view of the world (Spence, 1982; Viderman, 1988).

Humanistic and Integrative Version of Truth

Humanistic approaches also maintain that it is subjective experience that matters most, but rather than trying to explain it, they emphasize the need to understand it. Humanistic approaches try to facilitate the process of intensifying a person's experience, expressing, articulating and clarifying it, aiming at acceptance and understanding. They contend that personal truth matters and that it is in the process of discovering this that value lies. The type of research that goes with this model of truth is that of process research. It is not surprising that these types of approaches encourage the most diversity, with truth being defined as a function of personal creativity and choice. They have led to the practices of eclecticism on the one hand and of integrationism on the other. The former takes the view that diversity of method should match individual difference and preference. The latter holds that we need to arrive at a principled integration of all of this diversity whilst retaining breadth. The challenge of finding a standard of truth under these conditions becomes ever greater. Pluralism can easily lead to a lack of discipline. But as though the search for truth in this field were not difficult enough, there is the additional complication that all of these approaches can be applied to work with adults, children, adolescents, couples, families or groups and that in each of these situations different norms and standards apply. One can imagine the myriad of claims of effectiveness and the difficulty in assessing truth.

The Need for a Meta-model of Truth

My view, which I have argued elsewhere (van Deurzen-Smith 1988, 1990, 1994) is that the only way forward through this maze of human inventiveness and intervention is to go back to the basic underlying philosophical issues. Before rushing into defining the skills, competencies, methods or standards of practice we need to be reasonably clear on the following points. What is human well-being? What is mental health and hygiene? What defines quality of life? How do people lose track of these things, how do they regain them and how can they maximize them? What, in other words, are the existential parameters that make living either possible and worthwhile or impossible and meaningless? How can we establish truth in this area, if we merely measure the outcome or observe the process of psychotherapy without addressing these more fundamental issues? It is like comparing the relative prices of foods or the quality of their packaging before we have determined what kind of diet is healthy or whether the foods in question are nutritious and non-toxic. If we do not address those basic points, the results of our work can only be haphazard and at times dangerous. If psychotherapy and counselling concern themselves with people's moral, emotional and spiritual well-being, as I believe they inevitably do, then we had better begin by establishing of what this consists. If we want to open people's minds to some greater truth about themselves and the world, then we must have some notion of what that truth is.

Let me give the somewhat disguised example of the struggles that one particular young woman had in finding truth for herself. It will illustrate the need for some kind of overarching framework of values and truth by which people can orientate their lives. This is needed, not just for the sake of psychotherapists and counsellors, but for the sake of survival of our culture, which is currently in danger of beaching itself on the arid shores of post-modern nihilism. The time when it was possible to prescribe to people how they should live by reference to authority or faith are long over. The truths by which people live their lives these days are more likely to be self-generated, subjective and often ephemeral.

Irma's Predicament

Irma was a young woman who sought psychotherapy when she was in her late 20s and had been married for seven years. She was most attached to her husband, Jim, and had made considerable sacrifices in adjusting to his way of life and view of the world. He was a naval officer and she was a musician. She was inwardly contemptuous of the life of external appearances that her husband required her to maintain but into which she had nevertheless settled. He, in turn, had made considerable sacrifices to her way of living and she was aware that he often felt confused by the uncertainties with which she confronted him, when she questioned his view of the world or asked him to be more sensitive to her needs.

They had succeeded in creating a cocoon of shared reality out of the considerable challenges that such differences inevitably bring. He eventually gave up his navy career to take on the captaincy of a commercial ship, so that he could be with Irma more often. She was unemployed and was able to travel with him and sometimes sing with the band. Most of the time she felt restless and useless and before too long, on one of their long sea voyages, she became attached to another musician with whom she felt she could at last communicate on the same level. This began to crack the carefully constructed protective shell around Irma and Jim as their shared reality was challenged.

It took a long time before Irma was able to establish a version of the truth that would permit her to force a separation, something that she felt an urgent need to do in order to maintain her self-esteem, which had been badly eroded in the marriage. The fact with which she was faced was that they had, for seven or so years, done everything in their power to bring their lives and views of the world together and more in harmony with each other. Irma's identity was shaped around the resources that had been available to her. It was only now that she had begun to feel safely ensconced in her marriage that she could open up to the realization that many of her abilities remained unused, leaving her feeling of no value.

Irma had compromised what mattered to her to such a large degree for the benefit of the couple, that she would eventually have to either perish or come to reclaim her own truth. At the same time what she had shared with Jim mattered greatly to her, as it seemed to be all she had and as she had made such sacrifices for it. She could not suddenly simply abandon it. She was in such a bind that she became depressed to the point of being unable to function. She then entered psychotherapy and began to adjust her view of herself and her position by re-emphasizing certain aspects of her experience, whilst allowing other aspects to become obscured or even forgotten. She was used to maintaining the tensions in the marriage by thinking of herself as being able to influence her husband's way of commanding his vessel by, for instance, advising him on which bands to engage. Now she began thinking of herself as having been caged on the ship because he wanted to keep her to himself at all times.

Instead of seeing herself as having an opportunity to compose during the many moments where her services were not required, she began to think of herself as playing second fiddle to him. She cultivated a vision of herself as victim of the relationship and soon found that the truth of their mutual commitment to each other that they had shared to this point became easily undermined. She discovered that once this process of erosion had begun and her new version of reality had taken root, a rapid crescendo followed and she began looking upon herself as having suffered a kind of martyrdom for the sake of their joint happiness. The sense of self-righteousness that came with this vision of having sacrificed herself spurred her on to search for ways out of the relationship. When such a change of attitude takes place, an opportunity for consummation usually soon arises, and indeed Irma at once succumbed to the charms of the bass player on the ship, who encouraged and confirmed her new version of reality. The affair that followed promptly led to the dissolution of the marital relationship.

Psychotherapeutic Interpretations

Some would assume that Irma was immature for not being able to sustain her relationship to Jim and would implicitly encourage her to stay in the relationship no matter what. Some would assume that her depression was a sign of deep-seated psychopathology and they might even consider her incapable of ever relating satisfactorily to others. Others would claim that Irma was simply lacking in self-esteem or self-assertiveness for sticking it out for so long in an unhappy marriage, letting her husband dominate her. They might encourage her to take quite drastic action.

As long as we do not have a clear measure of what is right and wrong in personal affairs, it becomes a matter of opinion whether an aspect of behaviour is seen as strength or weakness, health or illness. We do not have standards for moral and mental well-being in the way we do for physical health. It is much harder to establish what keeps a person happy than it is to establish what keeps a person healthy. Physical health is directly correlated to survival, whereas it is quite complex to determine the relationship between personal conduct and long-term benefit. But it is not impossible to do so. You will remember my daughter Sasha's discovery that a certain type of relationship to truth had certain personal consequences for her. Similarly, Irma discovered that her change in attitude had far-reaching effects on her.

When Irma had construed her situation as one where she had to suffer and fit in, she became so constricted that she could not function. When she construed her life as so limiting that she should break out of it, she became capable of action again, but found herself to be rather destructive. She felt that neither of these ways of looking at her position was ultimately entirely right and, in a search for truth, she decided that she had to test her view of reality against that of Jim, rather than leave him in a huff.

The two of them now started a long process of trying to establish a shared view of the truth of what had happened. This allowed Irma and her husband eventually to separate on amicable terms, each deciding to go their own way. The joint account of the truth about what had gone wrong was that Irma had been too dependent on Jim and that she was too needy to be able to adjust to the demands of naval life, whilst Jim had been too narrow-minded and lacking in empathy for Irma's soul to accommodate her artistic inclinations.

Fifteen years later, both had developed this compromise of truth in rather disparate ways, as they no longer had any contact with each other. At this point, fate brought them back together and they had occasion to hear each other's version of reality as it had by then developed. Irma had become a rather successful musician, with several recordings to her name, whereas Jim was still working for the same company. Both had remarried and had a family of their own, neither was left with too much resentment about the past.

Irma was shocked and amazed to find that her ex-husband believed himself to have been oppressed by her magnificent musical talents and had come to believe that he had been utterly dominated by her at the time. Irma, whose memory of her first marriage had become increasingly focused on the sense of having suffered constant humiliation and lack of recognition for her personal talents, was at first unable to relate to Jim's account at all. It felt as if there had been two pasts that had been lived by two sets of Irmas and Jims.

While Irma knew that there was not much hope that Jim would ever agree to her version of what had really happened all those years ago, she realized that she would gain greater truth for herself if she could in some ways accommodate Jim's version as well as her own. What she discovered was that truth does not necessarily coincide with strongly felt subjective experience, neither does it necessarily lie in the exact middle between different versions of reality. She also realized that Jim's sense of their past relationship threw a new light on it, brought out some of its hidden truth, that neither she nor her therapist had been able to detect at the time. This new insight was strangely strengthening to her. It allowed her to question herself in new ways and to see that while she had thought of herself as weak in the past and mostly strong in the present, it was not really that clear-cut and there might have been an implied strength in her weakness in the same way in which there was a hidden weakness still in her now that she was strong.

The objective truth of what happened between Irma and Jim could never be fully established, even if one had been able to send out 20 independent recorders observing them throughout their marriage. Our conception of what is true is modulated and amended over time and alters in the light of changing circumstances. Jim could not have thought of Irma as his many-talented oppressor if she had not escaped from him and developed her talents. Had she remained with him, then her truth that he belittled her and kept her under his command and at his mercy might have been borne out: for then she would not have been able to develop the talents that he now took to be part of the picture.

Multiplicity, Complexity and Relativity of Truth

It is with personal reality as it is with history. Both are defined after the fact and in relation to the outcome of the situation. It is the victor who writes history and who determines our particular angle on the "truth" of what happened. Truth in this sense is not so much like a woman, or a man, but more like a child, that keeps growing into something different and gets constantly redefined and amplified over time. This also shows how complex and relative human reality is and how vulnerable psycho-therapists and counsellors are regarding truth because of this.

Recent controversies over the falsification of memory that may be generated in psychotherapy have abundantly demonstrated that psycho-therapists and counsellors have the almost impossible task of navigating between Scylla and Charybdis. On the one hand lies the danger of ignoring the hidden truth of clients who have experienced severe trauma, who have been unable to face it and who continue to avoid speaking the truth about what happened. On the other hand lies the no lesser danger of encouraging romantic versions of reality that could go as far as the creation of false memories and invented truths that lay blame on innocent people and may lead to unwarranted and unjust actions.

How can we steer clear of this dual danger and find a course through the narrow opening of truth into safer and clearer waters? The answer must lie in determining what the dangers of untruth are. It is only by observing what can go wrong in human living that we begin to get a sense of the open space of truth. Each individual's experience enlightens our search for truth about human existence and adds a piece to the puzzle. If we keep ourselves open to being constantly challenged and corrected by the effects and long-term consequences of people's actions, we are more likely to find a truth that will guide us in the right direction. We have to let subjective or theoretical interpretations be contradicted and expanded by different views and seek the overarching principles that can encompass them. Commitment to a larger truth allows people to transcend personal troubles (O'Hara, 1986; Baumeister, 1991).

Deconstructing Truth

This makes it all the more disconcerting to note the post-modern tendency to dismiss the possibility of discovering any valid universal truths. As cultural relativism, social constructivism and deconstructionism dominate the field of the social sciences and humanities, we urgently need to ask ourselves how we can accommodate these perspectives and go beyond them. As I have already shown, there is a salutary aspect in deconstructing established notions of truth and health. It provides us with an excellent starting point to our investigation. But a radical deconstructionist attitude leads one to debunk and unmask any claims to truth and any contentions of ultimate value to such an extent that we are left without a foothold in reality.

It seems to me that this nihilistic attitude is exactly the one that psychotherapists and counsellors often encounter in their clients. It is very much a sign of the times and the logical outcome of a consumerist and anthropocentric view of the world. This attitude considers truth to be the product of human invention rather than something based on ultimate laws. Baudrillard, for instance, says that "the secret of theory is that truth does not exist" (Baudrillard, 1986, p. 141). Derrida claims that "There is no such thing as a truth in itself, but only a surfeit of it. Even if it should be for me, about me, truth is plural" (Derrida, 1979, p. 103).

It is all very well to take the post-modern stance of the little boy who shouts that the emperor's new clothes are not really there and claim that truth is just a human construct. All that this achieves is the undermining of the search for truth. The emperor may be stark naked, but he is nevertheless still truly there. We cannot be let off the hook of our investigations so easily, even though it may be extremely sobering and beneficial to be reminded that much of our so-called "knowledge" and "truth" are nothing but make-believe.

Art and Science

This should not discourage us from pursuing an improved version of truth in a scientific manner. Neither should it stop us from continuing to apply our understanding in an artful way to enable people to make sense of their lives and create meaning for themselves in ways most in keeping with truth.

Bowlby (1979) in his essay on "Psychoanalysis as art and science" made the interesting observation that our discipline needs to be both art and science. Unfortunately there are too few psychotherapists and counsellors who take the science part very seriously, preferring to hide in the art of their everyday practice. This may be because there has been a misunderstanding about the science in question. As long as it is psychology, psychiatry and statistical analysis that are peddled as the relevant sciences, psychotherapists and counsellors who daily deal with the human predicament will rarely find science relevant to their work. It is the science of living that is our subject and that science is certainly not an exact one.

Wooing Truth

Nietzsche was not so far off the mark when comparing truth in this domain to a woman. If Nietzsche was right, then we would be a lot better off facing our impotence: this woman has not been captured or understood and what is more she never will be. Like Heraclitus' river that keeps streaming on and is therefore never the same river twice, life flows on in ever-changing patterns and we cannot capture it, but only learn to live it.

This should not become an excuse for an anti-intellectual and relativistic attitude and we should have the courage to admit how little we really know. It is only from the starting point of admission of our ignorance that we can begin to work in the right direction and systematically study what has been so long neglected. T.S. Eliot summed it up rather well:

Because I do not hope to know again
The infirm glory of the positive hour,
Because I do not think,
Because I know I shall not know
The one veritable transitory power.

(Eliot, 1930, "Ash Wednesday")

No amount of pontificating on the part of psychotherapists and counsellors will teach us anything until we submit our speculations to the universal laws of human existence. No amount of human culture will shield us from the facts of life. If psychotherapy and counselling are disciplines to safeguard human well-being, it is time that we come off our high horse and begin a simple, basic and systematic investigation of what makes for a good human life.

To do so means to take a stand and at the same time to accept that every understanding is also a misunderstanding. To search for truth requires us to be open and transparent, vital, personal and at life's disposal. It means to venture, to search and to dare be in error and stand corrected in the good old tradition of scientific investigation.

If truth were only a woman or a man, if truth were merely human, it might not be worth risking oneself in this way. But for my part I am convinced that truth is much more than human and I am quite content to submit myself to it, instead of trying to elude it. In a post-religious, post-modern society, truth, in my view, is the only guiding light. In my final analysis, truth is life.

HARD-EARNED LESSONS: THE THERAPIST'S OWN JOURNEY TO SELF-UNDERSTANDING

It is hard to admit that your therapeutic work is sometimes harmful rather than helpful. It is even harder to see what exactly you do wrong. It is hardest of all to actually learn from your mistakes and put the experience to positive use. Only time will allow you genuinely to reap the benefits of new insights and implement them in your work. People can take many years to really assimilate new ideas and counsellors are no exception to the rule.

While preparing to write this chapter about some of my own mistakes, I was struck by how much I could learn from events long past. The wisdom hidden in each situation is released in small doses as and when we are ready to read the message. Lessons drawn from the same experience will vary over time, according to the new perspectives that we acquire.

The key to the learning, however, remains the same in all situations: it is that of candid reappraisal. One has to give up the proud belief in one's own knowledge and expertise and accept situations in their embarrassing detail and complexity.

I offer the following illustrations of my personal struggles with an overriding sense of relief at speaking the unspeakable. I have tried to set the learning in context without finding blame, either in myself, in others or in situations. My own quest for answers and my discovery of questions is illustrated in the following case examples, encompassing 25 years of therapeutic work. If I have learnt anything during that time it is to have a greater capacity to spot errors and sustain my own and other people's scrutiny of them.

Death: the Great Supervisor

My first experiences of therapeutic work took place within the setting of psychiatric hospitals, where I practised counselling and psychotherapy first in a voluntary, then in a professional, capacity. I was in my early 20s and had studied philosophy rather than psychology, although psychoanalysis had been included in the curriculum. My attitude to my work was one of great optimism and I had more than my fair share of missionary zeal. I saw the therapeutic challenge as an opportunity to make the world a better place and I was filled with the conviction that it was possible to help people straighten out their lives, no matter how confused or perturbed they were.

The first hospital in which I had a full-time post was located in the middle of the French Massif Central. It had been a place of revolutionary progress, which is why I sought it out. It was the first psychiatric hospital in France to break down its walls and allow all patients to come and go as they wished.

As the hospital was situated in the mountains with no major urban centres within a radius of 100 miles, there was little incentive for people to run away. On the contrary, there was all reason for them to remain, as the hospital was organized as a therapeutic community, enabling patients to participate actively in all aspects of its life. Some of them were in positions of leadership in the print shop, the woodwork shop, the kitchens or the laundry. Others were instrumental in the social activities which were the centre of the hospital and village life.

With so little cultural activity in the area, the hospital was the point of reference for the staff as much as for the patients. During the two years that I was a resident therapist, I spent most of my evenings talking and drinking, dancing, organizing games or playing boules with patients, doctors and nurses. It was a fascinating time and I learnt a tremendous amount from my personal relations with patients and staff alike. Just observing the senior therapists interacting with the patients taught me more than I had previously learnt through any other form of training.

Some patients had been there so long that they liked taking the new therapist aside to teach her about their problems and how to get a handle on them. The camaraderie was great and I was at the receiving end of a mixture of old-fashioned respect for someone with a university degree, on the one hand, and parental concern for someone still so young and inexperienced, on the other. On the whole this made for a fairly comfortable learning environment.

There were times when things were less rosy and I was forced to confront my own naivety and ignorance. One of the reasons for this was that I had been catapulted into a role of leadership for which I was not yet ready. As the wife of one of the five psychiatrists in the hospital, and with my philosophy degree and two previous years of psychiatric work behind me, I was expected to fill the gap left by a previous registrar's wife. She had been a group analyst and she and her husband had been the linchpins of the hospital's progressive therapeutic community programme.

Amongst other things, they had created an internal radio station and a weekly newsletter. Through these media anyone could say anything, no matter how controversial or offensive, on the condition that they come to the weekly meeting where the issues were aired and discussed as the newsletter articles were read out aloud and commented upon. These two-hour meetings took place on Saturday mornings and were the occasion for intensive sessions of group therapy. Fifty to eighty patients usually attended, accompanied by perhaps five nurses and three psychiatrists. The Social Therapy Centre, which was responsible for organizing the meetings, had three staff members, two of whom had had intensive training with the therapists who had created the system. Within weeks of my joining the team I was asked to take over the management of the meetings and I accepted with a mixture of pride and trepidation. It really was a case of fools rushing in where angels fear to tread.

Although the other staff and the registrars were usually quite active at these meetings, and although we had regular debriefing sessions afterwards, I often felt terribly exposed and sometimes unable to bring difficult situations to their best conclusion. The human distress and upset that was revealed in the newsletter articles was such that I felt constantly pushed to the edge of my human security. I used to tremble with anxiety every Saturday morning, and it was only my strong desire to do well that allowed me to believe that, no matter how terrible the patient's situation, there always was some way to understand and tackle it.

Interventions by most of the team were based on a mixture of psychodynamic principles and common sense (the latter flavoured strongly with the rough and ready morality of the French countryside). There was also some psycho-dramatic input and sometimes a more directive behavioural one. The overall trend was to challenge people and encourage them to take charge of their own problems and speak their minds. I easily became convinced that shaking people out of their complacency was generally a good thing, as I often saw them finding a more satisfactory place in the communal life after having a go at writing a newsletter article and having their difficulties publicly confronted.

Nevertheless, there were numerous occasions when I was shocked at the way in which particular patients were brutalized by this rather forthright way of tackling very private matters, and I had a tendency to smooth ruffled feathers and ease tensions with rather moralistic and calming remarks. I did not have the poise to conduct the sessions with the authority required to keep people's emotions on an even keel. I doubted my own insights and pandered somewhat to the greater knowledge and experience of the senior therapists, who criticized me for being too intellectual, too scrupulous and too guarded in my approach. They rightly considered me naive, idealistic and unequal to the task of dishing out home truths in the way that they believed was necessary. To them I was the privileged, learned stranger from the city who needed toughening up.

There was undoubtedly some truth to this view and I felt self-conscious about my therapeutic role, given this context. At the same time I was aware that my youth and sensitivity (as well as my sense of alienation as a foreigner) made me more able to appreciate the experience of the most withdrawn patients. I felt far better equipped than many of my colleagues to understand some of the young schizophrenics who were often sent down to us from Parisian hospitals as a last resort.

In one-to-one work I trusted my own insights and abilities with these people. But the public group sessions with their culture of questioning and confrontation were a different matter. I was acutely aware that the interpretations offered were relative to the background of the therapist, but even so I did not have the strength or confidence to balance the interventions made with those based on my own perceptions. I needed some proof of the validity of my views before I would feel at ease with them and ready to stand by them. The proof that I needed came in a very costly manner.

One Saturday morning, as I went over the articles that were up for discussion at the meeting, my attention was drawn by the writing of one of the regular contributors. Marcel was a very withdrawn, intellectual young man who had been sent down to the hospital from a private clinic in Paris, where he had been unable to make progress. He usually wrote dry and totally impersonal articles that seemed to warrant very little discussion other than an invitation to express himself more personally. But today, here it was at last: instead of describing the beauty of the Roquefort region, Marcel had mentioned his personal preoccupations. What he described was his dismay at his parents' disapproval of his relationship with Sophie, another Parisian patient.

Marcel and Sophie had been seen walking hand in hand around the hospital for months now and everyone considered them a steady, though somewhat oddly assorted, couple. They seemed to love each other madly in spite of what Marcel's parents considered to be an incompatibility of their social backgrounds. He was from a well-to-do family and she was a simple working-class girl. Now that his parents had officially disproved of the relationship and had told their son to put an end to it, Marcel wrote in the newsletter to announce this fact in quite a melodramatic way.

Predictably, he was forcefully challenged by some of the therapists to speak his own mind rather than hide behind his parents' views. This did not help him to articulate his own views, but it entrenched him in a defensive position.

Sophie, who was also present at the meeting, was visibly shaken by the situation and I felt an urgency to let her viewpoint be heard too. I drew her into the discussion, intending to help her express her sadness at being abandoned. She was not able to master the force of her own and Marcel's emotions, however, and joined in with the general tendency to speak scathingly to Marcel. Before long, a violent quarrel had started between Marcel and Sophie, each shouting in mad anger at the other. I was at a loss to handle the situation tactfully and felt rather overwhelmed by the force of the emotions at play.

Some of the other therapists responded with excited exhortations to both Marcel and Sophie to tell each other the truth about their feelings at last. I was aware that many of my colleagues considered the situation a breakthrough for both patients, who were at last expressing feelings which were normally held very tightly in check. My intuitive sense was that this was no positive gain and that destructive forces were at work that could eventually only confirm those two in their usual state of withdrawal. I did not have the confidence to trust myself. Even if I had, I would not have had the authority to bring an explosive situation back under control.

Marcel worked himself up to unexpected levels of hateful and furious abuse of Sophie, in a pathetic attempt to show everyone how he himself, not his parents, dismissed her as a possible partner. He called her the most odious names and aired all his frustrations with her: he threatened her physically to make her leave the room. Sophie, although giving as good as she got up to a point, was finally cowed into marching out in anger. No one dared intervene. The therapeutic culture interpreted the situation as an achievement; Marcel was even congratulated on having spoken his mind at last. I felt like a failure for not having been able to keep the situation in perspective, but I let myself be convinced by my colleagues that I was too soft and that I should learn to actively bring about such situations regularly.

It was not until later that evening that people began to worry about Sophie, who had not come back to her ward. Late that night a search party was sent out to look for her, and by six o'clock the next morning Sophie's stiffened body was found in a nearby swamp. Accidental death was recorded: she had wandered into dangerous territory and had slipped. The metaphor seemed cynical and tragically appropriate to what my memory had recorded. To me this was no accident. I felt deeply guilty for having stood by and let her be challenged to death.

Others, too, did some soul-searching as the post-mortem meetings went over the facts again and again. But the fault was generally seen to lie nowhere in particular, or perhaps mostly with Marcel's parents. People were not willing to really question the therapeutic methods that had been employed. It was only over the months and years to come that I reclaimed my guilt and started to draw some conclusions. All the supervision I had on this case tended to whitewash my role and minimize the responsibility of any of us who had been there that day. Taking responsibility meant questioning the whole set-up of the hospital: even Sophie's death did not appear to warrant such a price.

But I found that I could not progress in my own professional development until I questioned *my* role in this tragedy. I needed to face my previous lack of understanding of the large group process before I could start noticing some of the forces that had been at work. I needed to recognize the narrowness of my thinking about human emotions before I could begin to make sense of the apparent contradictions of the events of that day. I needed to acknowledge how I had held back from intervening, even though my intuition told me clearly what was wrong and what would be right. I vowed that I would develop the necessary strength to stand by my intuitions.

Most importantly, I needed to accept that I had, by my own standards, failed miserably to be in charge of the group meeting: for only then was I free to begin recognizing and defining my professional values and goals. I discovered that there was a force of complacency and inertia in others and myself that inclined us to shirk all responsibility. Everyone was protecting everyone else from learning anything from the situation at all. It seemed easier to soothe the pain of Sophie's death by pretending that it had been inevitable. But I found that in the end I preferred the pain of feeling some responsibility for my failure, for it alone could lead to the hope that I could also have a positive impact and become truly effective in my work.

I learned that if I were to embark upon such a road I needed to sharpen my theoretical knowledge and my understanding of the human predicament, as well as to gain lots more personal and professional experience and grow stronger and more insightful. Without this, I could not work to the level of which I knew myself capable. I also decided that I would rely less upon human opinion to guide my work and more upon the facts of life. The reality of Sophie's death had proved to be the ultimate and only supervisor worth relying upon.

Knee-deep into Regression

After those first few intensive years of learning the profession, I decided to go back to University to get a first degree in Psychology and a Masters degree in Clinical Psychology. I had now moved to a new hospital, less experimental in nature, but equipped to provide me with more intensive and in-depth one-to-one work and regular supervision with a well known Lacanian psychoanalyst. I also attended seminars in psychiatry and psychotherapy offered through Bordeaux University, which introduced me to the use of phenomenology in psychotherapy (Binswanger, 1963; Boss, 1957). This brought together my previous philosophical research with my clinical practice and set me on the track of my future pursuit to base counselling and psychotherapy on a firm philosophical foundation.

With the accumulating weight of experience and training I began to experiment with new therapeutic methods that were in line with the approach that most interested me: anti-psychiatry. One of the problems with working in an anti-psychiatric manner was that the work of Laing (1960, 1961, 1967) and Cooper (1967) said practically nothing about practical application, so the descriptions of regression work in Berke and Barnes's book (Barnes and Berke, 1973) became the only available guideline.

Much of my counselling in the new hospital emphasized couple and family work. My then husband and I worked as a psychiatrist–psychologist team and we did much of the counselling and therapeutic work together, taking many novel initiatives within the hospital. We inevitably came to a rude awakening as we experimented with new methods without quite knowing what we were playing with.

We had just started to work with Hélène, a young mother of two, who had arrived at the hospital after a serious suicide attempt. She was deeply depressed, but very eager to take up the psychotherapy sessions that I offered to her after the initial assessment interviews and tests. It soon became obvious that she experienced her relationship to her husband as a major obstacle in her life. She felt incapable of coping with his demands on her as a woman, a wife and a mother.

It was therefore decided by the team that couple counselling would be more helpful, and my husband and I saw the two of them for numerous sessions, both together and separately. Soon Hélène was able to leave the hospital in a much more optimistic frame of mind, whilst continuing to return with her husband for twice-weekly marital therapy sessions. The husband, however, began to feel increasingly threatened in these sessions. This was hardly surprising, as it must have been quite obvious that both therapists believed that he needed to make some important adjustments to accommodate his wife's needs.

With hindsight, I think that we sided unashamedly with the perceived victim in the situation who, after all, was our patient. Whilst intending to help her become more independent, we encouraged her to evaluate the situation as untenable. The husband was rather insensitive and was also occasionally violent to her and the children, so it was difficult to like him. Nevertheless, it would have been preferable to have tried harder to get to the bottom of his frustrations. Instead, we more or less dismissed his desire to see his wife behave "more normally", as he used to put it. We naturally and wrongly assumed that we needed to protect her and made that clear in our interventions. The whole situation was a good example of how one's theoretical and personal beliefs bias one's views of the situation and, therefore, one's interventions.

The couple therapy finished before long, as Hélène and her husband decided to begin divorce proceedings. We were a bit taken aback by this rapid development and questioned ourselves vigorously on what the couple might be acting out for us. None of this questioning threw much light on the situation, as nobody (including our supervisor and other colleagues) had an inkling of the developments that were soon to follow and that we had undoubtedly ourselves helped to shape.

As soon as Hélène lost her husband's support, she turned to her therapists for support. None of this was rational or explicit: the fact of the matter was that she simply collapsed and had to be hospitalized yet again. But this time she let herself go into a deep state of regression, clamouring for our continuous and sustained care and attention. To our dismay we saw her lose all control over her own emotions, throwing tantrums, going manic, getting withdrawn, etc. etc. Eventually, she remained in her bed, soiling herself and needing to be spoon-fed.

I was seeing her nearly every day, but formal counselling sessions were out of the question. Our anti-psychiatric notions were being put to the test sharply, as we were tempted to resort to simple psychiatric diagnoses and treatment to fix the situation and make Hélène behave "more normally", exactly as the husband had wanted. There was a time when Hélène went mute and refused to communicate directly to anyone. Nevertheless, she stood close by when the team discussed her and she threw a shoe at us when we talked about her in what she perceived to be a demeaning manner.

I tried at first to be tolerant of her regression, but the fact was that it did not seem right or necessary for her to be in such a terrible state of dilapidation, no matter what the anti-psychiatry books suggested. The nurses did not appreciate the constant hassle and extra work, changing her sheets several times a day, and they were very concerned about her psychotic state. I gradually became convinced that the therapy had to take a new direction. Rather than helping her to get in touch with more and more intense levels of feelings, and rather than helping her make connections with past experiences of her sense of inadequacy and inability to communicate, I began to talk to her about life and how to survive it.

There is little doubt that I improvised desperately and furiously in order to get out of what I instinctively sensed to be a potentially lethal failure of my own work and Hélène's life. I abandoned all the professional timidity that used to hamper my work. I no longer tried to make interpretations or reflect back, or show empathy of any kind. I merely spoke my mind and in the process accused myself of having encouraged her to regress in this way. Somehow, Hélène saw the reality behind my words and grasped the urgency of my meaning. I refused to see her so often any longer and resumed seeing her twice weekly, urging her to come to the consulting room again instead of lingering on the ward. The whole team was in agreement with this new line (which in fact they had been in favour of from the start) and Hélène was weaned off her regression within weeks.

Over the next months she behaved like an adolescent girl discovering her own budding maturity and she became involved with another patient in the hospital in a very intense manner. It was eventually decided that it would be best for her to go to a halfway house for young women, rather than try to live on her own with her children. It seemed that Hélène really did need to find a way to stand alone in the world before she could tackle all the demands of adult life. When I left the hospital she was established in her new life with a fair amount of confidence. Even so, I wondered whether the situation could not have been handled more effectively at an earlier stage, reducing the losses she and her children suffered in the process.

My trials with Hélène had a great impact on me. It was only gradually that I could admit to myself all the doubts I had about my work with her. The experience taught me the importance of a sober and sound appraisal of a client's predicament and the value of finding a personal and level-headed way to intervene, based upon a realistic rather than an idealistic view of the world.

I also discovered that the encouragement of regression may be based upon and inspired by a therapist's desire to be needed and to have a visible impact. I came to see regression as often counterproductive and largely a function of one's inability to help the client cope with difficulties more constructively.

Therapeutic Delusions

I decided to leave the psychiatric hospital environment to come and work in London with the proponents of anti-psychiatry, not long after my experience with Hélène. I wanted to find out how to handle situations like this more expertly, and to learn as much as I could from the only professionals I still admired for their controversial writing.

My husband and I were invited to come and work within a residential therapeutic community and do some work at a crisis centre. In the process I learned that my remaining illusions about professionals' privileged knowledge and insight into people's suffering were, indeed, illusions. This experience also confirmed my view that it is important to intervene on the basis of one's insight into life and from a sense of one's own struggles with life: in other words, from a personal rather than a theoretical position.

It was my work with Philip that became the turning point of my understanding. Philip was a lecturer in his 60s. He had a breakdown during his holiday in London and had walked naked in the streets and shouted at people in the public library. He was in a state of great upset and excitement. He did not want to be locked up in a mental hospital but he recognized that he needed some assistance. When he arrived at the crisis centre, he had mixed feelings about the place. He insisted that people there did not understand him or appreciate the fact that the world was on the edge of disaster.

Philip was preoccupied with time going by and he was convinced that the world was going to come to an end soon if he was not able to rescue it. He would call emergency services or stop people on the street to let them know that they needed to help him to save the world. On one occasion he tried to set fire to the crisis centre. His presence was extremely disturbing and frightening to another guest at the centre and it was exhausting to the residential therapists, as Philip did not sleep at night at all.

It was because of this that my husband and I were called in, to relieve the team and help with the sort of behaviour that we had rather a lot of previous experience dealing with during our years of work in mental hospitals. When we arrived, Philip had finally gone to bed for a rest. There was an atmosphere of terror in the house and the therapists told us that they did not think it wise to try and keep Philip going any longer without medication or hospitalization. Besides the residential therapists, there was a team of two therapists who worked with Philip in daily individual therapy sessions. These sessions were conducted in a Neo-Kleinian fashion, with strong and repeated interpretations concerning Philip's desire to destroy the breast out of envy of his mother; his fear of the imminent end of the world was linked by the therapists to his fear of retaliation from the father. As we began to spend hours and hours with Philip we were to gain direct insights into his own evaluation of these interpretations. We were to find ourselves interacting directly, without the protection of a professional role, with Philip's bright, enquiring and critical mind.

Our first encounter with Philip occurred as he stumbled down the stairs, head-first as if he was trying to kill himself. He said that he had gone blind and had fallen down helplessly. Over the next two days he was to maintain this blindness as if he was shielding himself from having to face the world around him. It turned out to be a device that became the linchpin of his coming to terms with his distress. While the official therapist team interpreted Philip's blindness as a denial of his Oedipal desires for his mother, Philip was much more interested in discussing with us the far-fetched nature of such an interpretation. The idea that he had fancied his mother and felt aggressive towards his father was neither familiar nor helpful to Philip, but the Oedipal metaphor used in a more concrete sense was. As someone well-versed in Greek mythology, Philip was quite ready to recognize the connection between Oedipus blinding himself when he couldn't cope with the facts of life and his own temporary blindness.

He asked us to help him to write a manifesto to be put out in all public libraries, announcing the need for all mankind to work together in order to stop the world from being destroyed. Then he burnt the manifesto with us, asking us to make sure we would "burn the I's" that figured in it. We laughed with him about the implications of what he was saying: that the personal, or the eyes, had to be sacrificed, in order to achieve the saving of mankind. It was clear that, although Philip resented his own impotence in not being able to do more about the state of the world, he also recognized the need to move away from a strictly personal perspective on this dilemma. Rather like Oedipus, who made a personal sacrifice in order to save Thebes, Philip was seeking to find a way to be significant to mankind in the face of the nuclear (and other) threats that he felt so acutely aware of.

Making interpretations to him about his personal guilt in relation to his father and mother was not helpful. He would come out of his therapy sessions with the psychoanalytic therapists, filled with fury against their neglect of his personal meanings. He would fume and glare and say he did not want to screw his mother and therefore did not feel guilty about this. But when I gently suggested that he did obviously feel guilty about some things, he would come back to a calmer mood and a willingness to explore his real guilt and sense of impotence in saving mankind.

We discovered together that awareness of guilt implies understanding about right and wrong and therefore also shows a way forward for the future. It slowly began to dawn on him that there might be more constructive things to do than blinding himself, setting fire to a house or getting undressed in the street. He began to search for more positive ways of having an impact, especially in relation to his teaching job.

It was obvious that Philip craved the ordinary dialogue that took place between us, exploring the things that mattered to him and from his point of view. He was scathing about the so-called "deep psychotherapeutic work" that he was going through at the same time, for it seemed to him that this denied his reality and skated over the surface of his experience in order to make interpretations that seemed alien and clichéed.

It was in my work with Philip that I learnt to be true to what emerges in sessions with the client without trying to fit it into pre-established frames of reference. The struggle with Philip convinced me at last that I had to take this unmarked road with clients instead of relying on the theories in books. As is so often the case in working closely with clients, it was my daring to go on Philip's journey with him that marked a change in my own life. When Philip was ready to face life again in a different and more courageous manner, bringing his discontent about the world into his professional life rather than letting it oppress him, I was close to doing the same thing.

What this meant was that I had to strike out on my own, away from the comfort of the institutions within which I had thus far practised. This move to independence would hold its own challenges and brought with it a whole new set of lessons to be learned.

Unexpected Limitations

In my personal life some important changes took place at this stage: my husband and I decided to separate after a year of intense crisis, and I opted to remain in Britain to work in private practice rather than remain in the therapeutic community and crisis centre or return to work in psychiatric hospitals. It was important to me to have the freedom to work in the manner I believed was right and I was fortunate in also finding a lecturing job where I could begin voicing, exploring and testing my ideas.

In this way I gradually worked out my own approach to the psychotherapeutic dialogue, which I began to call existential counselling and psychotherapy. Of course, there were many ups and downs in my work with private clients, but there was a definite sense that I was connecting with their true concerns. The trick, I found, was to balance a willingness to immerse myself in their preoccupations, with a clear retention of adequate boundaries in order to remain in charge and sane in the process. I got the hang of it quite well after a while.

What helped tremendously was to have brought my life in line with my beliefs and convictions and to have lived, alone, through the challenges that this involved me in. When I met David, who was to become my second husband and the father of my children, it was like a confirmation of being on the right path. Our relationship strengthened my sense of personal balance and security in such a way that my professional work improved more dramatically than it had done through any form of training. I felt increasingly on top of my work and ready to tackle almost anything.

Then my personal life-style brought me up against my limitations. It was my own desire to have a baby that shook me out of my growing complacency. After ten years of professional work I discovered that my devotion to my clients could suddenly come up against a whole new set of priorities, with tremendous consequences for what I would be prepared to offer them.

I had taken it for granted that I would work, from my home, with people who needed intense work and great attention, which I had no hesitation in providing, even though I always stuck to simple rules of time and space. When I became pregnant for the first time and began to feel tired and egocentric and inclined to retreat, I was working with one particular client who made me wonder whether I could cope.

Yet, when I decided to refer a number of my existing clients on to other therapists and counsellors because I wanted to cut down on the work I was doing, I kept Anne on because she seemed to need me more than the others. With hindsight this should have been the more reason to refer her on. Of all my clients, it was Anne who would cope least well with my pregnancy and childbirth. But it was my own inexperience as a mother that made it impossible to oversee the consequences of this decision.

When I was about eight months pregnant, Anne became restless and concerned about my impending absence. Anne had been referred to me after a breakdown and spell in a psychiatric hospital. She had begun to worry about not being able to cope again when I moved to a larger flat half-way through my pregnancy. With my impending absence to give birth to the baby, the scene was set for Anne to plunge into a second breakdown. She held herself together while I took a couple of weeks off to have my baby and when I returned to my work with her she collapsed.

The mistake I made was not to recognize that Anne needed alternative arrangements. I thought that I could handle seeing her up to the week of the birth and again almost immediately after. But although I did not miss more than two weeks of work (mainly because my work was my only source of income and I could not afford to take a longer break), the quality and amount of attention I had to offer so soon after the birth of my son was nowhere near what Anne needed. Anne herself was a divorced childless woman in her late 30s whose difficulties centred around a sense that she had failed to do anything worthwhile with her life.

Behind her feminist and career-minded facade she deeply hankered for a baby of her own. Her marriage had ended in disaster, her boyfriend did not believe in family life and she had banned the idea of procreation from her list of desires, blatantly unaware of her own instincts. My new motherhood threw up many bad memories for Anne, who was the eldest of nine siblings, and it brought out her desire to be looked after. Her feelings of helplessness overwhelmed her and I was useless because I felt myself overwhelmed by the demands of both my baby and my client. I wanted her to be grown-up and independent, while she wanted mothering from me. In addition, she was caught in the conflict between her suppressed wish to mother and her blatant desire to be mothered. I was at a loss to help her sort it out at that particular time, because I was myself too caught up in a similar paradox (wishing I could be looked after so that I could look after my baby properly).

Anne was prematurely forced by the situation to face some painful issues, that she might otherwise have been able to tackle more gradually.

She was also deprived of her already fragile sense of being able to rely upon others and she felt unable to cope alone.

She spent some weeks in a psychiatric hospital, during which time I did not visit her or speak to her once, as I needed the break as much as she did. When she returned she was frail, but willing to take a hard look at what had happened. We worked together for a further year, in twice-weekly sessions, making steady progress and coming to some understanding of the way in which she interacted with the world.

Then, when I moved to a different area, she chose to be referred on to a colleague. I did not go out of my way to offer her alternative arrangements to suit her well enough to make continuation possible. For although we had made considerable headway and she had moved to a position of much greater self-understanding and security, there was a shared sense of relief that she could now make a fresh start with a new therapist.

The lesson I learned from this experience was that it is crucial not to overestimate your own abilities, and that no matter how stable and experienced you feel, there will always be new life experiences that will shake you out of your world in such a way as to question all of your previous learning. If the issues you are newly confronted with dovetail with those of your client, then extra caution and supervision are needed.

Personally, I concluded that I needed to cut my therapeutic work to much more reasonable proportions while my children were young and while I also had considerable teaching commitments. I chose to indicate those limitations to future clients and focus on shorter-term work. I discovered this to have a positive effect on the work itself: freeing me of unnecessary pressures and responsibilities and making the framework so clear to clients that their motivation to get on with the work seemed greatly improved as a consequence.

Blind Spots

As my work has developed and I have matured, things which once seemed mysterious and difficult now often seem familiar and straightforward. As in every other profession, we tend to reach plateaux where it seems that we can oversee the whole of our professional territory. Of course, such complacency is inevitably challenged by encounters with unforeseen circumstances. Totally new aspects of old familiar issues can be revealed when you least expect it and before you know it you have been bamboozled by a new mystery.

I now look forward to such moments of being temporarily stuck, having understood that they signify the new opportunities to rediscover my own ignorance and the endless variations of human experience. I find it rewarding when such a situation occurs in my own counselling and therapeutic work rather than in supervising students and trainees, as this is inevitably closer to home and involves the shining of light in my own blind spots rather than in those of others.

My recent experience with Teresa is a good example of such a discovery and the removal of a personal blind spot as it interfered with my client's progress towards understanding of her predicament. Teresa was a mother in her 40s, who came to counselling upon recommendation of her GP after years of struggles with her son, Tony. Tony had lost the last years of his secondary schooling because of severe states of depression, which had been diagnosed as schizophrenia after Tony had to spend a couple of months in a psychiatric ward. Teresa had a deep sense of guilt about her son's difficulties, as he had begun to withdraw and get depressed around the time that her marriage to Tony's father was beginning to break up.

Teresa was sure that Tony had been disturbed by the constant fights between her and her husband, Richard, and she was worried that she had needed her son's affection too much when Richard had not been there any longer for her. Because of this, she had encouraged Tony to live with his dad after he returned from hospital: she hoped to make up for her possessive love of her son by sending him back to the father he had missed so much.

In the sessions we went over her sense of having failed and emotionally abused her son. Both Teresa and I were used to Laingian ideas and we operated from the implicit assumption that disturbance in children is often related to the pressure on them from their parents. I unquestioningly assumed that she might indeed have been harmful to her son, even though I am generally sceptical of the current fashion of seeing child abuse everywhere. I helped her to work on gaining autonomy and we focused on her strong attachment to her own mother, but the problem with and alienation from her son persisted. We were somehow missing the point.

Teresa dutifully tried to keep herself distant from her son and let him be free of her and she reported instances of her struggles in doing so, against her better instincts. She seemed to expect approval from me at such moments and it became evident to me that she was operating from the belief that I wanted her to behave in certain ways. It also became more and more clear that such behaviour did nothing for her and nothing for her son.

It was only when she reported that her son had become extremely angry with her one day over a petty incident that the scales fell from my eyes. How could I have missed the paradox in the situation, how could I have been so blind to the obvious deceit in the relationship?

One look at what was actually in front of us revealed much more than all our previous attempts at analysing the situation. For here was Teresa, desperate with held-back love and longing for her son, anxiously avoiding any expression of her care and concern for fear of damaging her child further. And here was Tony, lonely and ill-at-ease at his father's, assuming that his mother had wanted to get rid of him, because he had been too much to cope with for her on her own.

Tony had never once complained that he had suffered from his mother's need of him. It was worth checking what he had in fact experienced. Not surprisingly, it turned out that Tony actually felt that his mother's love, when it had flowed to him, had on the contrary kept him alive and hopeful in the face of the fights and divorce between his parents. It was only when he perceived his mother as rejecting him that he began to feel deprived and insecure.

When Teresa began to show her affection to Tony, plucking up the courage to reveal her struggles and doubts to him, Tony began trusting her enough to tell her about his predicament over the past years. He had identified with his father and had withdrawn into himself as his father withdrew from the house. He had seen his mother's attempts at not imposing her love on him as a distancing manoeuvre, indicating that she wanted him out of her life.

Feeling thus abandoned and forsaken (by both mum and dad) had made him want to die, and he had attempted suicide in the hope that this would matter enough to his mother and father to bring them back together. As he noticed that it drove his mother even further away, he became more depressed.

Teresa was amazed that well-intentioned acts had had such a negative impact. She was also moved by the way in which Tony tried to help her to see how she had alienated her husband with similar attempts at leaving him free of her. At this stage Teresa's counselling sessions began turning around her difficulty in acknowledging her need to love and be loved, and we uncovered her reluctance to let others know of her longings.

Her son's communication to her had broken the ice of her self-deception and it had penetrated through my therapeutic blindness and collusion with Teresa's presumptions about herself. How often do we carry on colluding with clients' negative beliefs about themselves and the world without there being an outspoken and rebellious suffering teenager to point the way? I dread to think, and I am grateful for the quirks of life that show up the blind spots and cul-de-sacs that I get caught up in.

Obviously, my insight into what Teresa was doing wrong, once again, had its resonance in issues that were alive for me at that time in my relationship to my own children. I, too, had to learn that to give love as freely as one wishes, without reserve or fear of being abusive, is often kinder for the child than holding back with well-meaning non-intrusive but stifled affection. Being truthful about one's love also implies showing one's need for the other and sharing apprehensions and self-doubt. Although I had long learned this to be crucial in adult relationships, I found it harder to be confident on this score with my children, assuming that I had to protect them from confrontation with my human weaknesses. What I discovered was that it was preferable for them to have overt exposure to my limitations rather than being covertly condemned to them whilst labouring under the impression of my superiority.

My own learning coincided with Teresa's. And this confirmed another growing conviction, namely that productive therapeutic work inevitably stretches the therapist beyond habitual responses and patterns of living. Good therapy alters the therapist's outlook as much as the client's and until this process of mutual impact and reverberation has begun the work remains superficial and glib.

Conclusion

In all of the situations I have described, what was needed most was to take a good hard look at what was actually present in front of me. It is remarkably difficult to take stock of a situation and genuinely see what is there. It is ridiculously easy to be led astray and soothed into the false and fatal belief that you understand, when actually, with all your experience and know-how, you are still engaged in thinking in patterns and applying formulae.

What comes out through all five instances I have given above is the sense of being bound by my personal circumstances. My learning is tied up with my private interests and personal preoccupations. While these shine a particular light on the client's issues, they often at first stand in the way of my understanding, especially when the client's struggles parallel my own, which seems to be predictably the case.

I now mercifully recognize that this is not a tragic failing on my part and that it does not simply occur through lack of training or insufficiency of personal analysis: it happens inevitably because I am, beyond training and self-understanding, bound by the same existential dilemmas as my clients. It is a fact of life that we are never perfectly equipped to help others and we are never exempt from the human condition in which we intervene.

I would go further and argue that it is precisely because we share the human condition in all its contradictions and imperfections with our clients that we can be of assistance to them. We would become incapable of being of much help if we weren't ourselves deeply engaged in the fight for survival. What a relief to renounce the striving for perfection, once we realize how insufferable we would be if we could achieve true superiority, sainthood or a state of total self-knowledge.

My experience illustrates only too clearly that it is just as dangerous to think yourself above and beyond your clients' troubles as it is to feel overwhelmed by them. In my five examples I have illustrated both ends of the spectrum, and in each of these situations it was the client's distress or process that eventually pointed to a solution. The times when I came to the edge of my understanding were thus the very times that the clients' issues showed the way forward.

So let's be grateful for the clients who don't fit our formulae and patterns, the ones who fight us and make life difficult for us. Let's count our blessings for making mistakes, for these are the moments when we get thrown back into chaos and disarray, when we lose our foothold and are forced to stretch beyond already acquired knowledge and insight. For at the end of the day it is the error we remember and the easy success merely soothes us to slumber and dream our grandiose dreams of professional excellence and glorious omniscience.

Learning comes from seeing what is wrong and what is lacking. And one thing I have learned for sure is that I shall forever be lacking. I have faith in my own failures as guidelines to my work and because of this I can have similar faith in my clients' ability to learn from their mistakes. Instead of setting standards that neither they nor I can reach, the trick is to be fully committed to the opening up of the darkest recesses of experience. To let the light shine where darkness was is enough to keep on the right track and be challenged.

If we are to help clients to get a grip on the paradoxes that elude them, we must be prepared to be exposed to these paradoxes ourselves. In the process we will be subjected to continuous challenges and confronted with ever new aspects of human experience. Relentless self-examination and reflection are required to deal with them and make sense of them, when it becomes apparent that we do not yet grasp the full extent of our clients' difficulties. Together with them, we must expect to be faced by new complications and mysteries and we must be ready for a critical reconsideration of set ideas about life.

To me, it is this process of persistent reappraisal and questioning of what I am and how the world works that makes the psychotherapeutic profession so fascinating. It would otherwise be a dull and depressing job.

Therapy is about being human with other human beings and allowing them to let their humanity unfold. And if, as I believe, to be human means to err, we must have no compunction and false pride over erring, as long as we are willing to retrieve our steps and mend our ways as often as necessary.

I think that one of the things we need in counselling is more humility about our ignorance. Writing up some of my own mistakes and lessons learnt has shown me once more just how hard it is to have such humility publicly. It has been much easier in earlier publications (van Deurzen-Smith 1984, 1988, 1990) to recount cases where I felt some pride in my performance. Yet there is a curious satisfaction in mentioning the failures and letting go of the professional bulwark of pride and dignity. Openly admitting how biased and limited one is and how faltering and bumbling one's attempts at understanding life, is, to say the least, humbling. To do so and find peace with one's errors is strangely exhilarating. It is an experiment that I strongly recommend.

LETTING THE CLIENT'S LIFE TOUCH YOURS: THE ART OF RESONANCE
Rising to the Professional Challenge

The art of psychotherapy and counselling involves far more than applying skills, competencies or technology. It is generally recognized that practitioners are also required to draw on personal qualities and maturity, gained through life experience. There is much disagreement, however, over the nature or extent of such personal engagement with the therapeutic process. Some schools of thought teach that practitioners should be so well-analysed that they are able to separate their own material from that of their clients at all times. This gives practitioners licence to interpret anything that happens in the therapeutic relationship as essentially part of the client's material. The therapist is considered to be capable of anonymity and neutrality, of acting like a mirror, of being essentially absent as a person. While I believe it to be important that psychotherapists maintain sufficient distance from their clients' preoccupations in order to continue to have some perspective on them, I do not think it possible or desirable to focus on people's life problems without being directly and personally concerned about the issues arising.

There is to my mind no such thing as being fully analysed or being able to take a neutral stance. People are far too complex to make it a realistic proposition to even attempt to take such a superior position. As therapists and counsellors we are constantly tested and altered by life, just as much as our clients are. As I demonstrated in the previous chapter, just as we think we have safely achieved stability, we are confronted with new aspects of life that throw us off balance. Each time we are faced with the predicaments of a new client, this represents a new challenge which may startle us. The fact that our work with clients is done through the therapeutic relationship means that we are, by definition, placed within the narrow circle of their preoccupations, and we can easily be drawn into their areas of concern in a very intimate manner. As psychotherapists and counsellors we make our living through employing our own personality, our character, our life experience and ourselves in relation. As such, we put ourselves inevitably at risk.

We can minimize the possible impact on us by sealing ourselves off and pretending not to be concerned about our clients' issues, or we can respond by allowing ourselves to become over-concerned. I think that the hallmark of good psychotherapy and counselling is in being as deeply concerned as we can afford to be without losing our own bearings. We need to be fully available to the client and yet we need to be able to stand apart. We need to let ourselves be touched and moved and yet remain calm and composed. We need to know how to let ourselves be unbalanced and shaken and yet retrieve our equilibrium in order to provide the stability and level-headedness that the client requires us to provide at all times. This is a tall order.

Resonance with the Client's Concerns

It is not easy to deal with your clients' preoccupations with issues that are familiar to you because they resonate with your own past experience. We are never finished with the past and clients will touch off new aspects of what we thought we had mastered and understood. It can be even worse when clients draw you into territory that is a minefield for you at the present time. Sometimes it seems as if all your clients are going through the same sort of difficulties, all facing exactly the same sort of troubles as you are. The fact of the matter is that they often are. The human condition really is a fairly predictable one and we all confront the same issues sooner or later. It seems to me a good sign when you can identify with your clients' woes, for it shows that both you and they are alive and kicking. It shows that you are not blasé about the human predicament, but that it speaks to you loudly and clearly.

It is far worse if clients bring you material that is alien and unfamiliar to you and that you are not really willing or able to deal with in any depth. This is bound to happen sooner or later, for none of us is omniscient or omnipotent. It would be presumptuous to assume that we can ever be so experienced that we are familiar with absolutely everything. It is my contention that in all three situations, whether your client's problems resonate with your past, present or future preoccupations, it is possible to work well provided that you are willing to meet the situation directly. What I mean by "meeting the situation directly" is allowing yourself to struggle along with your client to make sense of something new and letting this struggle touch you in an immediate sense. It seems to me the essence of good therapeutic work to be able to engage frankly with the life problems that your clients are facing. The wisdom required to help another human being is not that of aloof superiority. Existential wisdom means being present to whatever comes your way and facing it resolutely. Psychotherapists need to be able to tolerate new problems and be steady when confronted with emotional upheaval. What makes you professional is not being unconcerned about the problems presented, but rather being adept at seeing through them and making sense of them.

What is required is not to stand above or away from your clients, having overcome your own difficulties, but rather to be able to face their human limitations as if they were your own, and to do so with all the strength and courage required to see it through.

Recognition or Resonance?

If you have this fundamental strength of character to bravely face new challenges together with your clients, it can be a distinct advantage that you are vulnerable to what is happening to your client. I personally find that I work best when I am myself deeply concerned about the issues that are acute for my client (van Deurzen-Smith, 1992). Note the distinction between being deeply concerned for my client and being deeply concerned about the issues that my client presents. To my mind it is an advantage to recognize the issues, whilst it is a disadvantage to identify too much with your client. If I am directly motivated to puzzle out some new problem that clients' troubles pose for me as well as for them, I work much harder and more effectively.

It is this that characterizes psychotherapy and counselling as existential for me, namely the recognition that my clients and I ultimately face the same predicaments. What my client is struggling with now, I have struggled with at one time, or am finding hard now, or will be confronted with in the future. None of us is exempt from the human condition. As therapists and counsellors we need to be capable of letting our lives be touched by those of our clients. It is no use occupying the high moral ground from which we can look down with mere empathy, interpretation or judgement: we have to struggle with our clients' problems.

The Search for Reality

In the final analysis, the extent to which you can be sincere and direct in the therapeutic search for understanding with your clients makes all the difference to how much progress can be made. It goes without saying that such realness is no excuse for getting in over your head, letting yourself become so fully immersed that you lose sight of any possible solutions. I am not suggesting that we need sympathy instead of empathy, but rather that there is room for a kind of "co-pathy", a recognition of being companions in the human struggle to live a worthwhile life under difficult circumstances. To make this an even more existential statement, one would probably have to reword it as "co-agency" rather than co-pathy, underlining the idea of us acting with our clients, together puzzling out this new enigma that is theirs, reformulating it in a cogent manner. In this sense we can redefine ourselves as our clients' colleagues in the job of living, partners in the solving of the mysteries of life.

When we function as therapist or counsellor we are, as it were, supervising our clients' daily lives and we do this with the concern of people who live daily lives too. We are with our clients in the struggle to survive this particular crisis or predicament as if we were facing it ourselves. Having the benefit of being once removed from the troublesome situation gives us sufficient distance to attempt to oversee it rather than getting submerged in it. We are co-workers, part of a team of two, looking together at the issues that one of us is currently confronting, but which are just as relevant to the other. We are subjectively involved in a conjoint study of the object of our mutual attention: that of the client's particular problem in living. In this process, what I had previously encountered becomes relevant to me in a new way as the client explores the matter with my assistance and begins to discover limits to living that I have not myself stretched beyond. Together, we try to survey and tackle whatever needs to be tackled and, while the client takes a particular way through the obstacles, I am at the same time making new connections and finding new pathways for myself. This allows me to make fresh and relevant interventions and can at the same time have dramatic and far-reaching effects on my own life.

There have been numerous times when clients have struggled towards a sense of what their priorities and values were, when I have suddenly slotted a new piece of my own puzzle of life into place and felt strengthened or questioned in a particular belief. No matter how much work I do on certain events in my life, they always remain a source of new inquiry. Although I have, for instance, talked *ad nauseam* about my various past migrations across Europe, leaving The Netherlands for France and later coming from France to Great Britain, I have still not exhausted the possible interpretations that these events can be given or the learning that can be gathered from them. I find myself inevitably reconfronted with a reconsideration of my own motivations and experiences whenever I encounter a client who is similarly preoccupied with having been uprooted.

Exposure and Protection

Recently I worked with a young Scandinavian woman who had settled in Britain after spending a few years in Morocco. She was perturbed about the fairness of her pale skin and the transparency of her almost colourless eyes. She had just had her hair cut extremely short to eliminate the final evidence of the dark dye that she had applied to her practically white hair in order to fit in with what she had experienced as a hostile and dangerous environment in Northern Africa. She sensed herself to be diaphanous and exposed and she remained nervous about being different from others, even in Britain. Although the distress she had experienced in Morocco was much eased, she still felt conspicuous for what she described as her "albino" appearance. She felt compelled to adjust, chameleon-like, to those around her in order not to attract negative attention. She was often stared at by strangers in public places, because she looked, in her words, like a freak.

In Morocco she had been unable to go anywhere alone, as she would otherwise fall prey to uninvited and unwelcome male attention. Her experience was that of being insufficiently protected by nature to deal with the onslaughts of the alien environments in which she had been forced to live because of her husband's job. The effect of constant sunshine on her tender and sensitive skin was equally devastating, confirming her self-diagnosis of being unfit to adapt to circumstances other than those of an isolated life in Lapland. The issues with regards to her relationship to herself, her Moroccan husband and her environment were complex and we worked on many strands of them.

Nevertheless, we would always return to her central concern with her physical inadequacy and I found myself strongly resonating with this. I remembered how frustrated and isolated I had sometimes felt when living in the South of France, feeling vulnerable for being taller than almost anyone around me and being singled out for looking nordic and atypical. It seemed to me, however, that I had never experienced this as a physical handicap, but rather as a social one. In working with my client during one particular session, during which we visited the territory of her extreme exposure to physical insecurity because of her inability to walk in the sun for fear of burning her eyes, I fleetingly remembered how the sun in the South of France had often irritated my own eyes. This recollection was a bodily one and I had not recalled it for years. It stayed with me powerfully during the next few days, as it was spring and my annual hay-fever was just starting. One day, after another session with my client, who was also preoccupied with the unusually hot weather and who also suffered from hay-fever, it occurred to me that my hay-fever had started when I was 18, which also happened to be the first year I lived in France. Letting myself be more drawn into my client's world of terror of sunshine, I suddenly vividly recalled the excessive eye irritation that had been the first symptom of my hay-fever, but which had been misdiagnosed in various ways for a number of years. It suddenly dawned on me that my hay-fever could have been an allergic reaction to the intensity of exposure to light that I experienced in an alien environment. I was constitutionally ill-adapted to that particular environment, but I had been hitherto unaware of that simple fact and I had found a myriad of other more psychological and cultural explanations for my unease.

I now felt true concern about my client's predicament, which consisted in her sense of being ill-adapted to the world she lived in. I could grasp her experience in a real sense, from inside out rather than from outside in. It no longer seemed a pathological preoccupation but rather an entirely sensible example of self-observation, sparked off by her instincts of self-preservation. I was now directly motivated to help her in her attempts to find a solution. I never told my client anything about my personal resonances with her story, although I actively went through a phase of retrieving personal memories of physical misery. My client did not need to know about what she had touched off in me, although I am sure she noticed, indirectly, that I became more aware of and resonant with her predicament and that I was more able to understand the poignancy of her situation and more keen to help her find her way towards understanding it herself. The process of this understanding was not one of finding fault or finding a causal explanation, but rather of trying to grasp the situational and physical implications of her experience in such a way that she became more certain about what and who she was, and what and who she could not and would not be. Gaining recognition for the difficulty of her struggle and her efforts to overcome it led to her being far more sure-footed and self-confident. This fuelled her explorations and search for positive solutions, and made it possible for her to open new doors to a world in which she could feel at home. My own journey towards a greater confidence in myself, through a reinterpretation of what I had myself experienced in the past, lit her way home.

Commentary

As long as we work from a medical model and consider the therapeutic situation to be about a healthy psychotherapist or counsellor intervening in the life of an unhealthy client in order to effect cure, we must conclude that getting drawn into the client's concerns must be seen as a form of contamination, and therefore as dangerously taboo. If we can shift our mode of thinking about the therapeutic relationship to seeing it as an existential investigation, then it follows that we can allow ourselves, or even encourage ourselves, to be open to wonder and doubt. We will then find that it is only as long as we can be questioned and shaken by our client's difficulties that we can even begin to investigate live issues. If we let ourselves resonate with our client's terrors and troubles, but also with their delights and comforts, we shall discover the ways in which all of these aspects of life hold a measure of truth for us personally, and how we can let ourselves be drawn into new and often fruitful investigations of what we thought we already knew. The secret of good psychotherapy and counselling is to know how to explore what needs exploring with both maximum intensity and personal involvement, and yet also with a maximum of alertness to the many angles and perspectives to the issue: examining it with a critical ability that the client is momentarily deprived of, through being too deeply immersed.

Those who consider this to be a rather too tall order would do better to stick to more skill- or technique-based approaches that give a firmer guideline for therapeutic work. If your practice of psychotherapy and counselling is to be based on wisdom and personal integrity, as I am proposing, this is not something that can be conjured up out of thin air. It requires life experience, strength of character and a willingness to be challenged that can not be acquired from books or training alone. This is not to diminish the importance of practical training or theoretical learning, for both have an important role to play in the process of becoming an accomplished practitioner. I merely want to emphasize that what I consider to be the essence of good practice is something more than can be gathered in this way.

Those who are best capable of standing in the tension of being real with their clients, without getting lost or drowning in their clients' sorrows, tend to be people who have successfully faced important challenges themselves and who have gained confidence in their ability to do so again, as I have described elsewhere (van Deurzen-Smith, 1988, 1990).

Firstly, such people are likely to have achieved economic autonomy and are capable of sustaining physical equilibrium, both for themselves and in their environment. Secondly, they are able to relate openly to all sorts of different people and they are likely to have had the experience of being directly responsible for others in some capacity or other. Parenthood, or care for a dependent parent or partner, are the most likely sources of this experience. Thirdly, they are likely to have encountered a number of significant personal crises, having faced loss and disillusionment and having overcome this with self-reflection and courage, leading to renewed vigour and self-respect. Lastly, and perhaps most importantly, they have a sense of perspective on the human condition, combining a recognition of cultural relativity with an awareness of the inescapability of certain universal dilemmas. Such perspective can be most easily gained from having been exposed to different cultures and languages and having had to survive in and adapt to alien conditions. It can also be achieved in other ways, through changes in class or profession for instance, but the toughest challenges by far are those of inter-racial and inter-linguistic movement.

Of course, all this experience needs to have been articulated and made available for reflection and understanding. This work can usefully be done in individual therapy during training, but the latter can never be a substitute for the essential experience and personal qualities themselves. If this all sounds a little too demanding, remember that none of us can muster the perfect ability and that perfection is by no means what is required of us. Clients are quite often more helped by our failures and faults than by our merits and virtues. They need to know we are human and struggling in the same way that they are. What matters is that we have a sense of direction and that we are actively on the way towards living life well.

This includes our ability to falter and fall short. Being real in the end is what it is all about. Trying to define what it means to be real inevitably defeats its own purpose, as we get sucked into abstractions and prescriptions and lose sight of the ordinary daily struggle with ourselves, our lives and our clients.

CAN COUNSELLING AND THERAPY HELP? DEALING WITH MORAL ISSUES

Dante's *Divine Comedy* begins as follows:

> In the middle of the journey of my life, I found myself inside a dark forest, for the right way I had completely lost.
>
> (Dante, 1307)

The predicament that Dante describes has much in common with that of many of the people who turn to counselling or psychotherapy today. People often describe a sense of being lost or at a loss when they consult a counsellor or therapist for the first time. Life seems intricate, intimidating and daunting to them, rather like Dante's dark forest, and they seek help in finding a safe path through it.

Dante discovered that his journey out of the forest led through hell and that there was no short-cut. Those who come for counselling or psychotherapy have no intention of whiling their time away in hell. Counselling and psychotherapy aim to provide people with the most efficient way out of their troubles and through their conflicts. This usually involves a process of clarification of clients' current predicaments, allowing them to discover for themselves how they can move forward.

This raises all kinds of questions. Is it really possible to help another person out of the dark woods of his or her personal predicament? Is it possible to show people where they can take short-cuts through life ? Can counselling or psychotherapy really help a lost person to find his or her way? Could the help given by the psychotherapist or counsellor take someone out of the frying pan into the fire, straight into Dante's inferno? Might counselling or therapy harm some people instead of helping them? On the other hand, do these professions do anything at all for people or are they a mere self-indulgence? If these helping professions really can help, of what does this help consist? How do you know when you need help? How do you know that you have been helped? Does needing the help of a counsellor or psychotherapist make you into a weak person or does it show moral strength to turn for help in this way? When is such help appropriate or relevant? Can we not get such help in other, better ways?

Why do we turn to counsellors and psychotherapists for almost anything under the sun today? Didn't we fare better before the days of the therapeutic? What is the use of this new therapeutic culture and what does it say about our society? More importantly, what does it do to our society? Could the culture of counselling and therapy be the cause of some of the symptoms it is trying to cure? May it be that this culture is ruining human relations, turning them into professionalized, jargonized stilted interactions? Or is therapeutic culture, on the contrary, at the origin of an ever-increasing self-understanding and an improvement in human relationships?

A Cultural Phenomenon

There are a lot of questions to be asked about counselling and psychotherapy and most of these urgently deserve to be asked. I shall sketch out answers to some of these questions but I hope that this will not stop you from asking further questions and join in the search for better answers. For, as counselling and psychotherapy gain more and more ground in society as independent professions, the doubts about their soundness and right to exist multiply as well. There are now 13,000 people registered with the British Association for Counselling and many thousands more who use counselling skills as part of other occupations, such as nursing, social work and teaching. It is a sure sign that a profession has taken hold when industry starts to take notice of it, and counselling has now reached the position where large companies have begun to routinely offer employee counselling schemes as a way of dealing with the stress that is costing the nation seven billion pounds a year in terms of lost production and sick pay (Buckingham, 1992). It has been suggested that counselling is the largest growth industry of the 1990s and it has now begun to touch all of our lives in one way or another. Psychotherapy shows a more modest growth, with about 4000 registered psychotherapists, but this profession too is rapidly growing.

Those who think that they will never need to go to a counsellor or psychotherapist may feel hounded by this new cultural phenomenon, which they regard as a threat and as evidence of rampant consumerism and self-indulgence. The press frequently expresses the doubts of the nation on this score and verbal attacks on counsellors and psychotherapists are now a regular phenomenon. The controversy is summed up nicely by Fay Weldon's quip that the organization Relate, which concerns itself with the counselling of couples who have relationship problems, should rename itself "Separate" (Weldon, 1994). Counselling and therapy are seen by many as an unnecessary evil that turns people into egocentric individuals who stand up for themselves but not for each other.

These new professions, which have become a public phenomenon without having gone through their paces in first acquiring legitimate status, are extremely vulnerable to such attacks. Counselling, especially, is all the more defenceless as it has been spread to a large extent through the work of an army of volunteers, who are often only summarily trained and who are not always best prepared to defend the profession in articulate and knowledgeable fashion. A large percentage of these volunteers are middle-class women who have finished raising a family. Counselling has therefore been grafted onto a number of existing battlegrounds, including the battle of the sexes, the battle of the classes and controversies over parenthood. As people frequently seek counselling to deal with precisely those same issues, one can imagine the potential fireworks when disagreements of value arise.

The profession of counselling has in addition attracted the aggression that is usually reserved for those workers who keep undesirable elements in society under control, and who become the recipients of the disgust intended for those they are meant to keep out of the way. It is a well-known phenomenon with social workers, prison officers or the police force, who become a target for violent disapproval any time their efforts fall short of the desired outcome, even though by the nature and object of their efforts they are doomed to fail frequently.

Therapeutic and Other Professions

Counselling and therapy are about assisting people to improve their lives by becoming more resourceful in living, but the very thought of having to improve our lives inevitably reminds us of our inability to lead satisfactory lives in the first place. Psychotherapy is quite often blatantly about helping people who consider themselves non-functional, or ill, or pathological in some other way. Most of us do not like to admit weakness or defeat and we do not relish asking for help in very private matters. For centuries we have turned to our families to keep us together in the secular world and to the clergy to keep us together in terms of our spiritual needs. With those two systems failing to function at the desired level, new support and repair systems are needed.

It is unrealistic and undesirable to expect this help to come from doctors. Doctors may know about our physical well-being, but more often than not their focus on our bodies prevents them from seeing our human needs. Medical training requires future doctors to harden themselves against human distress. It stunts rather than enhances human perceptiveness and sensitivity. In order to deal with physical pain objectively, doctors must avoid getting drawn into people's preoccupations with their general well-being or with their personal experience of distress. Medicine, set as it is in the natural scientific mode, is ill-equipped to deal with moral and psychological issues. Knowing how to diagnose acute appendicitis or treat hypertension is something quite different from understanding a person's conflicting motivations, convictions, aspirations or values.

Psychology and psychiatry are disciplines that come somewhat closer to addressing human distress, but they primarily deal with behavioural phenomena, focusing on the objective and normative, rather than on the personal and subjective aspects of distress. Many people avoid seeing specialists of the mind for fear of ending up with a mental illness label and with the intrusive treatment that often accompanies it. Psychology and psychiatry are therefore seriously hampered in providing the platform for a simple talking-through of human troubles when things seem to go wrong or get out of proportion. In addition, these professions require such long and specialized training that there are simply not enough qualified practitioners to go round. It is not surprising that counselling and psychotherapy, which are unashamedly about dealing with human distress and which are available in a wide variety of settings, are becoming a much more realistic option to fill the space left by the demise of religious and family values.

Even so, counsellors and therapists are stigmatized by the suffering they set out to deal with. They get very bad press from many quarters. A friendly journalist whom I encountered as part of my professional duties said: "I hate all this psychobabble and the whole interfering busybody lot of you—when I feel low I have a whisky or I screw my wife and preferably both." Experience tells me that this is a sentiment that the wife is unlikely to feel happy with and which may well lead her to seek counselling or therapy in a few years time. If she is able to find a good counsellor or psychotherapist, she may well learn about understanding her husband's motivations as well as her own and find ways of improving the relationship. If she gets a less competent counsellor or therapist, she is quite capable of eliciting and receiving one-sided support for her point of view and she may end up idealizing the therapeutic intervention whilst leaving her husband in a self-righteous and resentful manner. She is at the same time likely to claim that therapy saved her life. The husband's original prejudice against the profession will be confirmed and he may even accuse the professional of having destroyed his life.

The entire therapeutic profession tends to evoke strong responses. It is an activity that leaves few people indifferent. It intervenes in the closely guarded areas of our inner world and intimacy with others. It concerns itself with the questions that cannot be asked elsewhere, with the issues that are too embarrassing to be aired in public. It is private and somewhat secret, mysterious and intimidating. It is also essentially of the realm that used to be reserved for religion, womanhood and family life, and this makes it all the more taboo.

How did these professions come into existence and how was it possible that they should grow so rapidly? If we turn to Michel Foucault's analysis of the history of helping in the Western world (Foucault, 1961), we find that the medicalization of psychological problems was a relatively recent, no more than century-old phenomenon, which replaced the consideration of people's psychological problems as that of the domain of religion. But since Foucault's analysis the medicalization of human distress has given way to the phenomenon of psychotherapy and counselling, which consists of talking your way through your difficulties with expert help rather than getting treated for your troubles. We are witnessing the next phase of culture, which Foucault and others referred to as the post-modern era (Foucault, 1969). In post-modernity people no longer seek to be cured of their troubles, they seek to remedy the sense of a disappearing self. It is the era that Rieff speaks of as that of psychological man (Rieff, 1966).

A lot of distress is generated by post-modern society, now that humankind has reached a position of potential self-destruction through atomic war or overpopulation and pollution of the planet. Mass communication increasingly rules our lives, endangering personal relationships, whilst little solace is to be expected from the old structures that used to safeguard human values. People often feel that they have a choice between either becoming commodities themselves as slaves in the production process or focusing so much on achievement in producing more commodities that they will not have time to enjoy the commodities that they have accumulated. This is generally known as the rat-race: the treadmill of life in which we wear ourselves out trying to survive.

A New Priesthood

In the middle of the confusion of the post-modern world, counselling and psychotherapy have come on the stage, heralded as the new road to salvation. Therapeutic culture has rapidly insinuated itself into society to become an indispensable presence. Counselling is benevolently and sometimes overbearingly on offer to us, whether we like it or not. Of course, there is in principle nothing new about pastoral care. It exists in every culture. There are spiritual guides in every religion and in our own Western culture Judeo-Christianity has traditionally made vicars, priests and rabbis available for individual and family consultation, to ensure safe transitions through the jungle and maze of adult living. Religion in this sense is not just about believing in a god, but much more about being held together in one's worldly existence by principles taken from laws and rules beyond oneself. This is, of course, the original sense of the word religion, which comes from the Latin verb *religare*, meaning to bind together.

In our scientifically-based, industrialized society of the end of the millennium, the gods of our forebears no longer have the credibility they once enjoyed. We have become used to taking things apart and analysing them rather than bringing them together and seeing them in context. In this alienating large-scale world, the mass media have taken over the function of our churches and they spread the gospel of consumerism far more effectively than Christianity once spread the word of God through Sunday preaching. People are no longer held by spiritual values as much as by the secular values that are conveyed by the programmes that they watch on television. These are based on pop psychology and pop philosophy, one part common sense, one part experience and tradition and one part superficial interpretations of research. In a world that changes fast and that requires people to be on the ball if they want to succeed, humanistic values of self-assertion, self-sufficiency and personal success have imperceptibly and ineluctably displaced the traditional religious ones of caring for each other and sacrificing oneself for higher principles and for those whom one loves.

The surefootedness of the nation is no longer guaranteed by eternal and divine principles as generations imagined them to be, but rather by appealing to our most crude emotions and to rather primitive notions of pleasing oneself by constant improvement and expansion. This is all very well as long as one's life proceeds according to plan. But the fact is that the master plan presupposes a margin of failure: this world economy can only be run effectively as long as there are haves and have-nots. The down and outs of this world get little hope from being confronted with the promise of more food in the supermarkets and better cars on the road. They simply do not qualify for this consumer's paradise. Even those who do qualify may find that their material success is temporary. When crisis occurs, as it inevitably will, or when people have to make important decisions about their lives or make sense of their adversity, there is little solace to be found in consumerism. Many of us are dissatisfied with this narrow definition of well-being anyway, and we look for principles and values that may carry us beyond the crude pleasures of egocentric materialism.

Clients are, on the one hand drawn from the population of deprived and disenfranchised people and, on the other hand, from those who have temporarily fallen on bad times or who are in search of meaning for some other reason. In other words, all of us qualify for counselling or therapy sooner or later for none of us are exempt from going down or losing our way at some point. The therapeutic profession is working hard at creating a new basis from which to deal effectively with these issues. It has had to be created rather rapidly to fill the vacuum left by our lack of moral and spiritual conviction. Counsellors and psychotherapists have succeeded in drawing sufficiently well on the data of scientific research and on common sense humanistic values, to provide a convincing alternative to pastoral help.

Therapeutic Dogma and the Ethics of Self-centredness

It is, however, highly questionable whether this quickly assembled package of moral first-aid is satisfactory in terms of the world in which we live and in which we have to live for a few decades more and in which our children and grandchildren would hope to survive for quite a lot longer. The current message of therapeutic culture goes something like this: it is alright for people to need help sorting out their lives now and again. If you turn to counselling or psychotherapy you can expect to get support for your aspirations and at least some gratification of your need for approval. Counsellors and therapists are trained to approve of you as a person although they may disapprove of your actions. They will not interfere with your personal plans, nor advise you to take one course of action rather than another. They will encourage self-reliance and personal initiative, facilitating a move towards more resourceful and successful living.

A survey of the professional training programmes on which I have worked over the past 20 years, as either trainer, director or external examiner, shows that both trainers and trainees hold fundamentally charitable and humane values. They posit the desirability of leaving clients free to find their own way forward in life from a position of greater insight into their current position. The general assumption is that left to their own devices, people will come to know what is right and good for them and they will succeed in attaining this. The over-riding principle is that of being true to oneself and fighting for what is one's natural birthright: to get a fair share of the cake.

This clearly represents a revolutionary break with most religions, which propose that persons are best served by following the path indicated by the belief system itself, as laid out in some religious text. Spiritual systems are generally concerned with the overall well-being of a group, society or culture, leaving the individual to adjust to the common good rather than encouraging the pursuit of personal satisfaction, with the assumption that this will also be in the interest of others.

We can trace this shift in our way of thinking about the role of the individual everywhere in Western culture. An interesting example of it is the way in which stories that have existed for centuries get translated to the screen by the American film industry. An illustration of this is

Andersen's story of "The Little Mermaid" (Andersen, 1835), a tale about a frustrated mermaid who falls in love with a handsome prince and who decides to betray her water kingdom and her family for the sake of his love. She sells her voice and tail to a sea-witch in return for legs and sets off to woo her prince. In the original version of the tale, the mermaid does not succeed in marrying the prince, the *sine qua non* of her survival. She discovers that princes prefer girls who can speak and who do not suffer incredible pain in pursuing them.

In the Disney version, the little mermaid succeeds in seducing the prince and in marrying him at the last minute, securing her dreams and continued life. In Andersen's version the mermaid is, on the contrary, left bereft from having betrayed her parents and sisters, who then sacrifice themselves to give her another chance to return to life at the bottom of the sea. The mermaid has to kill her prince and his bride in order to save herself but, having been through the trials and tribulations of her earlier egocentric and short-sighted decision-making, understands that it is her duty not to kill for the sake of saving herself. She opts for her own defeat and demise over the death of her beloved prince.

The original story is a true tragedy, where human or mermaidly vanity proceeds irretrievably to its logical downfall, redeemed only by suffering and eventual sacrifice. The Disney version of the story teaches that small sacrifices of oneself will lead to one's dreams coming true. The moral is one of learning to have one's own way. The parents are not shown as the holders of any greater truth, but merely as the abusive and misunderstanding intruders who would, for the sake of their own vanity, interfere with their children's happiness. This, too, is a significant change: as individualism is the objective, parents are seen as the obstacles to, rather than as the facilitators of, adulthood. Adulthood is increasingly defined as that time when you are allowed to do your own thing.

The notion that people themselves can determine their destiny in ways that are profitable and beneficial to them as individuals is a reflection of the increasingly humanistic emphasis of Western culture. This idea has taken over from the previous belief that God alone can give guidelines for a person's life. It is an interesting phenomenon that the scientific revolution, by making religion suspect, has plunged humanity into the dark ages of egocentricity. We currently behave as if we are the centre of the universe, whilst science should have shown us by now that we are not the centre of the universe at all. The fact is that we have not very much, or very rigorously, applied our scientific thinking to the issues of the position of humankind in the universe or in relation to itself. The current chaos in the social world bears witness to that fact. It is rather ironic that some people want to blame counsellors and psychotherapists for creating that chaos and its concurrent breakdown of family and human values, when counselling and psychotherapy are the very disciplines that are beginning to address the issues, albeit in a hesitant and sometimes misguided manner.

Psychotherapy and counselling are no more than the product of the same problems that make them indispensable to post-modern humanity. But because these disciplines are so intrinsically linked to their social context they are sometimes blind to the issues they are failing to address. Counsellors and psychotherapists need to reconsider their proper place in culture and they need to begin thinking about the overall needs of our world and the place of individuals within it. The political and ecological dimensions of spiritual, moral and personal well-being need to be addressed directly by counsellors, rather than leaving these to fate or deluded common sense. As a discipline, the pscychotherapeutic profession should dare to see itself more as a form of applied philosophy and ethics, teaching individuals to question and examine their lives in a non-prescriptive, non-dogmatic, non-condemning manner. Counselling and therapy have the potential to play an important role in the next millennium as the secular alternative to religion. These professions will have to develop both their theoretical underpinnings and their conscientious monitoring of practice enormously in order to achieve this.

The Hidden Potential of the Therapeutic Professions

Counselling and psychotherapy need to face the fact that many of the positive effects of their practice are related to factors other than specific skills. It is now well-established that the effectiveness of counselling and therapy is more closely correlated to the personal capacities of individual practitioners than to the particular modalities of counselling that they practice (Truax, 1963; Truax and Mitchell, 1971; Shapiro, Firth-Cozens and Stiles, 1989). The extra bits thrown in by counsellors and psychotherapists are often the most useful ones (Yalom, 1980) and it is interesting to note how these often express the personal views and life experience of the counsellor, otherwise hidden behind the veil of non-directive person-centredness, task orientatedness or neutrality.

I remember how I went for my first sessions with a French psychoanalyst in the early seventies. Although the sessions started out as an exploration of my own potential training as a psychoanalyst, it soon emerged that I had a few other problems to contend with. The memory that stands out above all else is that my analyst eventually made it crystal clear to me that a full analysis would only be possible if I achieved economic independence. At this time, I was still a student and my financial resources came for the most part from my parents and my husband. It was a bit of a blow to be told that I was not independent, for I thought of myself as very emancipated and autonomous. I was also disappointed to be considered not yet ready for analytic training (with hindsight I was rather young, but it did not seem like that at the time and it was never mentioned as an issue). There was no real alternative but to take this view extremely seriously, especially as it was augmented by the demonstration in the sessions of the narrowly academic nature of my life, which lacked the maturity of involvement in the workplace.

My analyst also categorically stated that my relationships were rather exclusive for the moment, and needed to be brought into perspective by meeting new people of all sorts of walks of life, stretching my horizons and bringing fresh ideas and experience to me. I was shocked by this bit of enlightened common sense mixed with object relations theory and professional experience, but it stood me in very good stead. Instead of continuing to be a full-time student I immersed myself in very full-time psychiatric work, which hardly left time for formal studies at all. I was catapulted into a new universe that brought me so much stimulation and challenge that my studies became infinitely more real, less exclusive and far more interesting. My sense of usefulness and belonging in the world improved almost overnight and a revolution in my experience of myself was begun that took me away from ever wanting to train in psycho-analysis, instead opting for a pragmatic in-service training in psychotherapy.

The moral and existential guidance provided by my analyst on this occasion was overwhelmingly more significant to me than the remainder of his interventions. In fact, some of the psychological and dream interpretations that he made set me on wild-goose chases and gave me a sense of self-aggrandizement and self-absorption that were counterproductive. The genius of this analyst came into play when he dared to be true to his perception of my life's predicament: that of isolation in an arid intellectual circle and that of failing to support myself and lacking in human dignity. He could have cultivated my self-absorption and kept me in a long, interminable analysis, where I would have wallowed in the minutiae of the life of my soul, but he could not help himself but to function as my spiritual guide and recommend practical changes in my life that made so much sense that I have never looked back since.

These are things that counsellors and psychotherapists are not taught: they are not normally told to consider a person's overall well-being and to recommend basic priorities to be attended to, such as being able to be self-supporting; making an active contribution to and with significant others; taking time to be alone regularly to take stock of one's actions and thoughts; meditating on the wider meaning of one's life in the broad context of the world we live in; and streamlining what we do with the values we adhere to. Such guidance would be considered too directive and specific. Clients are supposed to know for themselves what is good for them. In reality, they often do not know what is good for them and neither does the counsellor or therapist.

Counselling and therapy sessions all too often lead to a short-term vision of the client's best interests. What we fail to notice is that this may be a case of the blind leading the blind, or rather of the blinkered leading the blinkered. The direction that we follow is often that of common sense or of the trend of the moment. Self-assertiveness, stress management and other fashionable techniques are presented to us as panaceas that will enable us to live happier lives. Many of these gimmicks sooner or later are flavour of the month with the media. They promise quick fixes from a perspective of consumerism and the purchase of commodities of comfort. We absorb this kind of standard whether we like it or not, and too many counsellors and therapists are inclined to encourage clients to follow the lead of the current bit of creative thinking about human relationships. The fact of the matter is that we do not know any longer what it means to live well—and therefore we are all too often doing therapy in the dark.

Therapy and Counselling as Applied Philosophy

We really need to ask ourselves some searching questions. Counsellors and therapists need to consider the possibility of setting themselves the task of seriously investigating what life is all about and what people can do to live it better, rather than jumping on existing bandwagons or limiting themselves to psychological theories. What do we aim for when working with distressed people? Do we seek to readjust them to the society that we live in, by following the lead of the present level of thinking and feeling, or do we actually wish to play a role in rethinking the sort of society that we might want to create and evolve and the part that we all can play in this? If we do aim for a process of rethinking, then psychotherapy is set in a very different perspective. Counsellors and psychotherapists now will have to take on a role of questioning ideologies and values, rather than taking the prevailing ones as the bottom line of their work. They will need specific training in thinking through moral and political issues if they are to help others to think clearly about these matters. They will also need additional moral strength so as not to influence people by preaching dogma.

Counselling and therapy training can focus on life issues and can show people how to actively investigate their own beliefs, values and attitudes towards these. Therapeutic training can enable people to recognize contradictions and paradoxes, logic and irrationality, prejudice and wishful thinking. It can clarify distinctions between motivation, purpose and meaning. It can encourage the study of the challenges with which life is likely to confront people, and teach them to get better at thinking through the implications and consequences of choices and actions. It can allow people to get more at ease with the business of living as an art and a science, rather than as a haphazard enterprise that one strikes out on with naivety and on a happy-go-lucky hope-to-survive basis.

This does mean that the study of counselling and psychotherapy are taken out of their exclusively psychological and personal context into a moral, political, ideological and philosophical one. I would personally add that such a study of counselling and therapy as a total discipline also has to address the spiritual and metaphysical dimension most seriously, for people gain much meaning from having a spiritual life. With a lack of well-thought-out guidance in this area, there is a tendency for people to resort to superstition and fundamentalism instead of reaching out for rigorous questioning and a commitment to working within the parameters of knowable natural and life forces. Counselling and psychotherapy have the huge task of encompassing the spiritual and the existential dimension in this way, together with the emotional and the personal and the interpersonal, for only if the new therapeutic professions can rise to the challenge of overseeing the whole of human life will they have a long-term future.

Conclusion

If you have followed my argument, you will see that there can be therefore only one conclusion to the original question. Yes, counselling and therapy help, but they do not help enough, not as much as they could help. Counselling and therapy do provide the privileged, much-needed and rare occasions for taking stock and rethinking in a person's life. People crave such sober places for reflection more than ever. Yet the way in which the therapeutic profession is currently framed may compound the problems that bring people to counsellors and psychotherapists in the first place. As counselling and psychotherapy are powerful instruments for reassessing a person's system of meaning, they can potentially be as harmful as helpful. The art and science of counselling and psychotherapy deserve serious attention in order to hone and improve them, making them into processes that can truly replace the dogmatism of religion, without falling into the trap of harking back to even earlier forms of wishful thinking, superstition and suggestion.

The future of our ideological well-being might well be in the hands of the psychotherapists and counsellors. We had better start thinking about funding their research and ensuring a future that is positive, although I would personally prefer it to hold ample room for paradox, doubt, conflict and contradiction as well. For if we are to be true to the human laws that we can detect around us, this much is clear—that no matter how good our therapeutic systems are, they will never cure us of life. Life is incurable, terminal and full of challenges and we had better accept this. Psychotherapy and counselling should never pretend to lead to the promised land. But equally there is no need for people to be lost in the woods of life or drown in its seas out of ignorance and inexperience. There are too many people who seem to be coping but who actually suffer from a sense of alienation most of their lives. The message they convey is similar to that of Stevie Smith in one of her poems:

> I was much further out than you thought
> And not waving, but drowning . . .

(Smith, 1983)

It is an outrageous state of affairs that there are so many casualties of post-modern society, including the nearly a quarter of a million people who try to kill themselves every year in this country alone. We need to take extremely seriously the role of counselling and psychotherapy in remedying the situation. The therapeutic profession needs to claim its proper place in the world of professions and will come into its own only if it is willing to take up its role of secular and post-scientific religion. The views promulgated by counsellors and therapists should be based on an analysis of an overall *Weltanschauung*, rather than on a narrow humanistic or analytic base, as I have suggested elsewhere (van Deurzen-Smith, 1988).

Therapeutic education needs to take up its role of preparing people for self and world before it specializes in training professionals to help others. A new and autonomous discipline and field of investigation has been established. I like to think of it as applied philosophy, but it is probably a little bit more than that and should perhaps be referred to as a new life science or a new science of living. Sometimes I please myself with the invention of a new word to name it, and I think of it as the science and art of *ontonomy*, or that which investigates and rigorously applies the laws of existence.

One can easily see how important it could be to teach the principles of ontonomy to our children, during the course of their primary or secondary education, so that as adults they would not have to be so clumsy at living. I know of some schools that already offer such courses on a small scale, with active workshops on how we can learn to understand ourselves, the world and human relations. The therapeutic professions and their underpinning life science of ontonomy are literally still in their infancy and have much developing to do.

It is time that we became serious about evaluating the way we live our lives and conduct our relationships, rather than leaving it for times of crisis only. We need to teach people where to look and how to look, how to be constructively critical and how to get a sense of perspective, how to doubt, how to question and how to query; in short, how to rediscover themselves and their world. Although it is a good thing that counsellors and therapists are here to help those who have got lost on the way, it would be much better if we could get to a position from where prevention and education were of the order of the day, rather than crisis intervention and cure alone.

The fact that psychotherapy and counselling is such a rapidly growing sector should make us sit up and take notice. We need to act now to ensure that resources are improved and taken to the necessary level of prevention and education. There are a lot of distressed and lost people out there. It is one thing to be there to help them, but it is quite another to ensure that there will not be ten times as many people in need in 30 years' time. May these efforts blossom into something that will help people to make sense of their lives in a constructive manner, getting a little closer to solving the riddle of what this whole business of living is all about.

4

PSYCHOTHERAPY AND COUNSELLING

WIDENING HORIZONS: UNIVERSAL DIMENSIONS OF THE HUMAN DILEMMA

As people of the different continents and nations are drawn together ever more closely in a world that appears to be becoming smaller, we urgently need to review our understanding of the human condition. We have a wealth of psychotherapeutic theory and experience at our disposal, but much of it is not relevant beyond that of local or historical circumstances. Many of the ideas and methods were generated by personal observation and they carry the hallmark of the bias of individual practitioners. This makes them into interesting and often poignant examples of private truth and gives them the power of personal conviction. Our clients sense the struggles we have been through ourselves and they are keen to learn from our experience, adopting our perspective on the world, often by osmosis and imitation. The way in which we retell our clients' life stories may be more satisfactory to them than their own account was, and so they accept our mode of operating and our viewpoint, often rather un-critically. If doing so serves them well and helps them to move forward, who could complain? However, it still begs the question of whether it is sufficient for us to provide people with attractive, but subjective, alterna-tive ways of viewing the world. It might be argued that we should be able to intervene in their predicament from a position of universally valid objective truth instead. It remains to be seen whether this is a feasible option. Let me tell you a story in order to illustrate my point.

Allegory of the Mountain

Once upon a time there was a precious stone on the top of a mountain and at the foot of the mountain, spread around it, there were a number of villages. Each village was named after the stone on the mountain, yet each village had a different name. One village was called the village of the mountain with the green stone, one was called the village of the mountain with the red stone, another was the village of the mountain with the blue stone and a fourth was called the village of the mountain with the yellow stone.

Villagers used to wage wars with each other over which name was the most correct, and many wise men and women had made their reputation by speaking or writing in support of any one of the different viewpoints. As the wars became fiercer and fiercer and led to much bloodshed, one day the four villages decided to solve their conflicts by having recourse to what they called "scientific investigation". Instead of continuing to fight over which colour the stone truly was, they would send a party of four explorer-scientists, one from each of the villages, to the top of the mountain and they, together, would find out what the truth of the stone was. The scientists did a formidable job and after many months of hard work came back down the mountain and announced to their villages that the ultimate truth had been discovered. The stone was white: indeed it was a diamond which merely appeared in different hues according to the angle at which light reflected in it. Now the villagers knew that they had been deluded and immediately a law was passed that obliged all the villages to refer to the stone as the white diamond from there on.

But although the people knew that the stone really was white, they could not help themselves but be more interested in the way in which it actually appeared to them, now as green, now as blue, now as red, now as yellow. Although they no longer waged wars on the other villages, there was increasing internal unrest within each of the villages. People's belief in their own perception of reality had been undermined and the internal, traditional values that they had held dear had been artificially replaced with external ones that did not seem nearly as satisfactory. They felt that they had to comply with the official version of the Truth, rather than being allowed their own relative and more narrow version of truth. They had been thrown off-balance because the core of their experience and the centre of their reality had been altered. It took many long years for these people to realize that the different perspectives that they had cherished for so long were what had given the rich colour to their everyday lives. The pure white light of knowledge was a poor substitute for the red or the blue or the yellow or the green atmospheres they had once breathed and bathed in and fought hard to defend.

Eventually they began to notice how the supposedly true white version of reality was actually nothing but another viewpoint, no more or less true than their previously coloured ones, although perhaps a little more comprehensive. If you stood close to the stone and examined it minutely it was a diamond and white. If you lived further away it was a prism and surrounded you with colour: a different colour depending on where you placed yourself. To dare to allow for all these different viewpoints, including the encompassing scientific one, was a greater achievement than to pursue the discovery of one exclusive Truth. The new challenge was to understand that the truth of the stone was multiple and varied and yet also one. But this was something that the people found hard to do. It was easier to stick to an opinion. It was personally satisfying to assert that the light of the stone was blue, or green, or yellow, or red or white. It gave you something to fight for and gave you a sense of belonging with those who fought with you.

So, in spite of their great scientific progress, the villagers of the mountain with the diamond remained in disagreement with each other over the true meaning and colour of the stone. Their scientific discovery did not make their life any easier, it merely shifted their preoccupations, took away their trust in their own views and added further dimensions of debate and disagreement. The peace was only restored when they began to admit this to themselves and when they were willing to explore the many different versions of reality alive amongst them. As long as they thought they could prove the truth, either by opinion or by facts, they missed the essence of what they were confronted with.

Their challenge was not so much to establish the Truth of the stone, but to learn to live with the mysteries of its many shades of light. To explore all of their different experiences and interpretations of the stone's reality was as valid and important an enterprise as to establish the stone's essential composition. To search, to doubt, to debate and explore and to keep altering their views and adding perspectives was all part and parcel of their challenge. They were only misled each time that they thought that they had found the final and definitive answer; the be-all and end-all. They only got lost or into wars each time that they stopped searching and doubting, debating and exploring. But even the positive action of the search and the exploration sometimes stood in their way of appreciating the stone and its whole spectrum of light. It prevented them from savouring the reds and the yellows, the greens and the blues, not to mention the purples and oranges, the entire rainbow of light. It interfered with their recognition of the miracle of the light itself, for which the stone, after all, was nothing but a prism. When they got too absorbed with the knowledge that could be had about the stone and its colours, they forgot to attend to the hidden wisdom and mystery behind it all. They neglected to attend to themselves and failed to be in awe: the wonder of living in the light of the stone was lost on them and had to be slowly retrieved anew.

Living with Mystery

The process of rediscovery of the mystery of life is difficult. We are more at ease worrying away at what seems wrong with life than we are at welcoming what is right with it. In our profession we are obsessed with cataloguing and correcting pathology, viewing others' predicaments from a standpoint of superior prescriptiveness, as if we knew the answers and were at leisure to change people's lives for the better if only they would conform to our view of reality. Our training does not prepare us to question *our* theories of life, or to imagine what it would mean to face up to different realities and circumstances than the ones we currently take for granted. We are just like the people in the villages of the diamond mountain. Some of our approaches say reality is red, others call it yellow or blue or green, or white. Nevertheless, we must accept that the hidden secrets of life that have been subject to interpretation and dispute over the years are still hidden beneath our conceited beliefs. On the one hand, psychotherapists have come up with a number of official versions of human reality, and have to some extent succeeded in enhancing people's ability to take control over their lives. On the other hand, such control is limited and comes up against the contradictory complexity of the human condition as soon as circumstances are somewhat out of the ordinary.

Especially when personal problems are set against a different cultural or political background, the limitations of much of existing therapeutic gospel become quite obvious. Psychotherapists are culture bound and they are biased by their own situation, which is personal and family-, class-, race-, nationality- and continent-specific. Human beings are limited and contextual and in our work with other human beings we are confined by our own outlook, no matter how broad-minded we think we are. We need to consider whether such a state of affairs is intrinsically harmful or whether it may be an advantage for our profession to accept that we have to continue operating in such a manner and learn to work with an awareness of our own prejudice.

What to say about the Western psychotherapist who makes continuous interpretations about the lack of ego-strength or autonomy in his Indian client, who is torn between her loyalty for her family and her desire to fit in with her cultural practice on the one hand and her objections to the arranged marriage envisaged for her on the other hand? What of another therapist's insistence that her Japanese client's preference for the law of her organization over her professional relations with colleagues are the result of failed object-relations? How can we move away from our tendency to judge and condemn and put human conflict and experience against a broader background of cultural variety and find new, more effective parameters for understanding our clients' preoccupations?

As a reaction to the growing awareness amongst professionals that particular theoretical accounts of reality are in fact biased and sometimes possibly harmful and abusive, there is a growing movement to integrate theories into a more palatable generic overall therapeutic model. The movement for a more scientific or integrative approach to the subject could be seen as the attempt to strive for the one single Truth that will explain all our difficulties and provide us with the facts of life. Our previous multifold individual psychotherapeutic theories and methods are the equivalent of the coloured views of the stone on the mountain; the scientific aspiration is to reduce all that to the discovery of the stone's diamond status.

The question is whether, in pursuing either of these lines, we have understood the real issues at stake. Psychotherapy is about understanding human life. In spite of all our glorious attempts at overcoming life's problems, and regardless of all of our scientific and technological achievements, living remains a daily confrontation with assorted challenges and obstacles. You don't have to be a psychotherapist to notice that life is an endless struggle, where moments of ease and happiness are the exception rather than the rule. Although there are some people who seem to take it all in their stride and who thrive on life, ever cheerful and positive, they are the clear exception and they often are an irritant to those who have to live with them. Reassuringly, even these super-people hit their Waterloo sooner or later. All of us eventually have to declare defeat.

Most of us find life really tough at the best of times and close to impossible when things start to go really wrong. As long as there is recompense for trying hard, we put up with this state of affairs and we make the most of the good times that we can get away with. Some of us flounder, however, and become bitter and aggressive, chronically depressed or cynical and withdrawn. All the many variations of these states have been amply and ably described as forms of psychopathology.

States of Dissatisfaction

We have developed a myriad of methods to alter those states and cure or treat those who have fallen into them. Some put the blame on genetic and physical factors in those who suffer, others prefer to look at these states as temporary illnesses caused by various internal and external factors. Some believe that the experience in the womb sets the scene for a person's mode of operating for the rest of life. Others consider the very early, infantile experience of people to be decisive in the way they will handle themselves later on. There are those who consider the whole childhood interaction with parental figures to be determining. Yet others put the emphasis on current patterns of interaction and put much of the responsibility of success with the present individual. Some emphasize the physical underpinnings of behaviour, others consider the cognitive dimension to be uppermost. Some take social conditions and demands to be crucial elements. Some underline the relevance of a spiritual dimension.

Faced with this diversity of views, most professionals who are at work in the counselling and therapeutic field today have been trained to become familiar with a combination of views on the causes of psychopathology. They are taught to inform themselves of all the various theories in the field, applying ideas as they seem appropriate to the case in hand. Various forms of psychotherapeutic integration or eclecticism have thus emerged.

We are so preoccupied with finding explanations and solutions for people's worries and difficulties that we rarely notice the premise upon which all this rushing around for health is based. Now and then some authors shake us out of our rut by drawing our attention to the possibility of a reappraisal of our usual assumptions. Yet such stimulating challenges to the status quo of the therapeutic culture still leave the basic suppositions unaltered. A division between those who cope and those who do not cope remains in place.

The Search for a Cure for the Human Condition

Psychotherapy has launched itself into the ocean of human misery as a raft that could rescue those in danger of drowning. It was built upon the belief that human misery is avoidable and undesirable, that it is the consequence of pathology and illness. Every form of therapy offers its own formulae to end the suffering and help those who are entrapped to escape from their prison of neurosis or psychosis.

People often hang on to the image of illness to capture their existential discomfort because it allows them to strive for health and improvement. There is nothing wrong with that in principle. We all seek solutions to the crying injustices of the human condition, and most of us long for some kind of utopia. We thrive on the image of mental illness, because it affords us the comfort of our own salvation in the harbours of mental health. Many are prepared to go through the illusory incantations of five-times-a-week analysis in order to gain access to the promised land, where no-one or nothing can any longer threaten their hard-earned status of total security in the lap of the luxurious knowledge that they are now one of a happy elite.

As professionals we know such aspirations to be illusory, as a truthful survey of human existence exposes intrinsic difficulties that cannot be overcome. Human troubles are clearly an essential part of life, rather than one of its anomalies or aberrations. We have to face the possibility that they are a constitutive part of living and cannot be eliminated. We are then obliged to ask ourselves whether this means that the more troubles we face, the more alive we might be, and whether the difficulties that psychotherapy tries to eliminate are in many cases the difficulties that we should instead learn to appreciate at their true value.

Reconsidering Our Objectives

Should we therefore aim to approach the matter differently and look for a global, over-all network of explanation that tells us what matters to all human beings, in any place or time, gaining secure insights into the difficulties that all human beings are confronted with sooner or later?

If we decided to do so, there are at least three essential sources for arriving at a broader view. Philosophy, when it is done as an inter-disciplinary meta-analysis of theories of living, can highlight and describe the human condition better than most disciplines. Anthropology, as it extracts the common denominator in all human variations, can guide our study of the underlying vital factors that inevitably return. Biology, especially the study of the brain and the human mind, in association with cognitive sciences, can provide us with a solid foundation for our obser-vations. We need to spread the basis of our studies in those directions if we are ever to make real progress for this profession and save it from being a mere fashion or momentary fad.

Is such an approach warranted? In order to answer that question we need to ask ourselves how we define psychotherapy and what its aims and objectives are. The word "psychotherapy" can be translated literally as "care for the soul", for in ancient Greek the noun *psyche* means soul or life-force and the verb *therapeuo* means to care for or to serve. In its original meaning, the word *therapeuo* is not related to healing, in the medical sense, but to the notion of caring for and looking after. A thera-pist, according to this radical interpretation of the old concept, is the servant, the assistant, the attendant. The client is the master, the em-ployer, the one who is being attended to. The psychotherapist, in the most literal sense, would therefore be the servant of the soul of the life-force.

Although the profession of psychotherapy has become rather mystified with sophisticated terminology, techniques and methods, we do not have to remain so alienated from the simple realities of life with which our clients are struggling. If we are truly to understand the soul that we are supposed to be looking after, then we must attend to the prospects, pur-poses and projects of this soul. Now that we have the paraphernalia of psychotherapy as a separate discipline with established training programmes, registration procedures and official recognition as a profession, it is possible to let this discipline come into its own. We now have a chance of succeeding in what we have failed to do for nearly a century of psychotherapy: to establish a true discipline of human existence, the blueprint for a systematic and practical wisdom.

Why should we turn to philosophy to find a new foundation for psychotherapy? The answer is simple. Philosophy is the love of wisdom. Those who seek psychotherapy are often lost and confused, disappointed, upset, stressed or distressed, troubled or disturbed. They need wisdom and understanding rather than cure. Currently in psychotherapy we forget to ask the moral questions or to recognize personal dilemmas as philosophical issues. We experience doubt and worry, anxiety and strain like every other generation before us, and we construe these experiences as abnormal, sick and undesirable.

But many of our clients' troubles are not about sickness or illness, but about ordinary difficulties in coming to terms with the obstacles that life throws at them. In this sense we need to have a greater insight into what such obstacles might be and how human beings have tried to overcome them over the centuries and in different places. The various philosophies and religions that human beings have developed in different cultures become extremely relevant in this case.

My own practice has been pinned on the writings of existential philosophers, who have particularly investigated such matters of life and death and who have tackled the moral and cultural questions that living in a reflective manner inevitably throw up. Heidegger, for instance, has spent most of his writing career formulating the essential ontological characteristics of human existence and he has urged us to recommence thinking about these issues. His emphasis on the importance of our finitude and the necessity of reframing our existence in light of the awareness of the passing of time has poignant resonances with the predicaments of anyone whose life is currently threatened. The moral of the story is that this applies to all of us, regardless of age, nationality and outlook.

Philosophy can teach us to question our assumptions and to reconsider the judgements we make about our clients' lives. I continue to find it a fundamental source of wisdom and guidance in my attempts to understand other people's experience. But I have also come to recognize that a constant reference to how the world actually operates in practice is crucial, if we are to not lose our way. The biological and physiological data of scientific investigations are relevant and need to be taken into account. It makes a big difference if I know that my client is likely to be affected by a particular genetic disposition, such as that of Down's syndrome, or if he or she is likely to have physical difficulties in achieving particular goals.

Universal Elements of the Human Condition

At the end of the day such knowledge might stand in the way of my true observations of my client's condition in human terms. If I get too specific and too preoccupied with the personal and the culturally relative I may lose sight of the overall perspective.

This overall perspective is most easy to keep track of if I turn to anthropological meta-studies, which tell me about what is valid for human beings of any origin at any time in history. It will provide me with a map of the generic human aspects that we all share and that make it possible for us to communicate and understand each other. It allows us to make distinctions between those things that are relative and those things that are valid for all of us. To make interpretations about life based on a knowledge of what is likely to be the case is a great deal more effective than to make interpretations based on one particular perspective.

It has been shown by recent authors that some of the original studies of a variety of cultures had been interpreted as showing more cultural difference than was warranted. Freeman published a book to show that Margaret Mead's study of adolescence in Samoa, for instance, had underestimated the difficulties adolescents experienced there as well, although it was handled differently (Brown, 1991). Relevant to our earlier metaphor, Berlin and Kay (quoted in Brown, 1991) showed that although anthropologists had believed for a long time that colours were perceived in arbitrary ways by different cultures, there are in fact consistent patterns of colour observation, which show that when a language has only room for two colours, these are black and white, that when there are three, red is distinguished in addition to black and white and that the next colour to be added is always green or yellow. Colour distinctions therefore evolve in universally predictable ways and cultural differences leave much room for a basic similarity.

Other more potent universals are things like: all societies are governed by the emphasis on labour and on the roles and status as they are distributed around human labour. All societies are built around rules for sex, affiliation and aggression. All societies define differences on the basis of distinctions between gender. All cultures are embodied in language and allot superior status to those who use it well. Language leads inevitably to the possibility of misinterpretation and the existence of gossip, it allows for humour and insult. It is always based on nouns, verbs and the use of the possessive. It is inevitably built on the juxtaposition of couples of contrasting concepts, such as good and bad. All cultures use language for story-telling, with the use of metaphors. All cultures have units of measurement, which are stable and can be translated from one to the other. All languages have units of time, where past, present and future are recognized as significant entities. All languages distinguish between generals and particulars and between certain logical notions such as affirmation and negation, same and different, parts and the whole. Emotions are remarkably similar in all cultures, and although some cultures exercise control over facial expression, they will respond in a more similar manner when believing themselves unobserved. In every culture there is a concept of personal responsibility, although it may be counterbalanced by a greater focus on loyalty to the group. Distinctions are always made between those actions that are under control and those that are not, although the value placed on either may vary according to cultural norm. All people are seen to have a private, inner life, with memories, plans and choices between different courses of action. All cultures acknowledge human development and its stages and crises: some have more complex systems to deal with them than others. All cultures recognize the importance of dealing with childhood fears. Copying and respecting elders, the importance of seeking shelter and the emphasis on the need for rules around mating are also universal human principles that are respected everywhere.

Reciprocity and rules for giving and taking are the guidelines of social relations; rights and obligations are recognized everywhere. Conflicts and sanctions to deal with these are standard practice. But though the principles remain the same, the variations on how all these matters are dealt with are great. What we can learn from all this is not to be over-preoccupied by either our own standard ways of looking at things, or to move towards the other extreme and consider everything to be culturally relative. We must seek to recognize the fundamental principles underlying our clients preoccupations and find the basic human elements in them. Only then can we usefully consider the various possible ways of tackling them. Not to be stuck in our own cultural modes of operating, but to be open to new ways of doing the same old things is essential if we are to serve our clients well. We have to make the effort of displacing and challenging ourselves. We have to see beyond our thus far limited horizons.

Conclusion

We need to complement our therapeutic work with a new sort of investigation into the essential aspects of human nature. The study of psychotherapy should broaden its scope and inquire into what makes human living worthwhile and the human condition acceptable. It is time for us to begin searching for the connections that exist between all the things that we know. We need to stop explaining their causes and instead enquire into the significance and value of it all.

To be a psychotherapist in an age of trans-nationalism requires us to have the breadth of mind to be prepared to be shown that our views are insufficient and incomplete and to start out anew. But we do need to keep a foothold in some reality and avoid relativizing everything, sinking into a pit of nihilism. In our opening up towards contrasting points of view, we shall discover that some things are definitely human and shared. The objective is not for us to harmonize and reduce the multiplicity of the human condition under one common denominator, but to learn from each other and recognize the diversity of human experience, which is both mysterious and miraculous and well worth paying attention to. We must stop holding on to simplistic and reductionistic single truths. In order to do so we need to admit our ignorance about human living and begin again from a standpoint of doubt and wonder.

WHAT IS EXISTENTIAL ANALYSIS? A SUMMARY OF THE EXISTENTIAL APPROACH

If it is true that philosophical approaches to psychotherapy and counselling might provide us with the kind of broad framework of reference that we need to do justice to the human condition, we have to look carefully at the tradition of existential analysis, which is the most outstanding example of philosophical psychotherapy.

My answer to the question, "What is existential analysis?" will be threefold. The first part will be personal. It will highlight what makes me personally interested in this approach and how I came to be attracted to it in the first place. The second part will be theoretical. It will scan over some of the philosophers who have inspired me, extracting a few salient points from each. The third part will be methodological and will review some of the guidelines for practice which I adhere to. Although I agree with John Heaton (1997) that an existential approach is essentially non-technological, I also believe that one needs some method, some parameters, some framework, in order to retain one's independence and clarity of thinking. I do want to stress that what I am going to say represents a purely personal view and that I believe that there are no rules or prescriptive formulae; the existential approach has to be created anew by each practitioner. All we can do is to give our personal views and bring these together in order to discover a little bit more truth about human living. Every view can only be partially true and therefore I do not consider what I am going to say as the Truth, even for me, but simply as part of my search for a way towards a truth or some wisdom. So let me begin by saying what makes existential analysis relevant for me.

Personal Aspects

When I was a teenager in the not-so-swinging sixties, I found it rather hard to live. What I discovered in the world around me seemed contradictory to what I had been expecting from the world. I was born some years after the end of the Second World War, in a country which had been overrun and terrorized and deprived of its dignity and resources, from parents who had suffered through hunger, loss and the sheer terror of living in hiding. When my parents started a family, in difficult conditions, it was with a sense of liberation and peace and a determination to make something good out of these new beginnings. The children they put into the world had to be raised and prepared for a better world. My early education therefore centred on hope, optimism and idealism, while much travelling in Europe was meant to make me a citizen of the world, with an understanding of different customs and beliefs.

Upon entering the adult world I found that the reality around me resembled the war images more than the peace fantasies. Although I never went hungry, the news was always full of others who did. The country was not ruled by the enemy but all the institutions I had contact with seemed to be. The struggles I witnessed my father going through in his work seemed just as bad as his accounts of the war—maybe worse, because his suffering was endless and had to be endured, while during the war he could resist and fight. My own experience in secondary school seemed an exact reflection of the same contradictions—working hard, against my will, on things that hardly interested me. It seemed that very little of what was being taught had any personal relevance. It was not surprising therefore that most people appeared to be unhappy and confused about living.

But of course there were some points of light. Some things did make sense and helped me in finding a way forward. First of all, there was poetry and there was literature, where authors were expressing the same concerns about life which preoccupied me. Unfortunately, the most relevant books and poems were rarely studied in class. Then there was music, which could focus, express or soothe emotions. Last but not least there was philosophy, which I discovered—mercifully at an early age—through my classical education and reading of Plato. Socrates became like a saviour to me—a role model, showing how it was possible to remain lucid about life's contradictions, to retain one's individuality and to stand up to a society which tries to deny the ideas that really matter. In many ways, Socrates and his method of philosophical investigation remain one of my inspirations to this day.

When I decided to study philosophy, I was deeply disappointed to discover the stodgy way in which the subject was treated in Dutch universities; this was something very different from what I looked for in philosophy. So I escaped to France where the events of 1968 had had a vigorous impact on the way in which the universities, and philosophy departments in particular, were organized. Marx, Freud and Lacan were studied closely. Although the history of philosophy remained important, input from phenomenology, existentialism, structuralism, linguistics and psychoanalysis was the order of the day. The political dimension of every philosophical problem was considered together with the personal and emotional dimension. Few professors dared any longer to teach dry and abstract theory.

I found that this type of study prepared me far more adequately for the work in psychiatric hospitals upon which I embarked at this time than the specific psychiatric training which I was also to take part in. But I was to receive the real challenge and the most effective learning when I took up my first residential job in a psychiatric hospital in the French Massif Central. This was an exceptional place, as I have described earlier, where no walls retained patients and where life was organized in an essentially communal way, with patients and staff all relying on the same village and hospital structures and events for their leisure activities, for instance. The contact with patients was close; philosophical dialogue was one of the established ways of interchange—not because this was considered therapeutic, but because it was relevant to some patients; they requested and initiated it, freely discussing their life's problems and their ideas about the society which had rejected them. The pieces of the puzzle started to fall into place. I began to understand some of the connections between my own sense of alienation and that of those who lived in the hospital. I wanted to know much more about methods of dealing with it, but neither the study of clinical psychology nor the psychotherapeutic training that followed threw any real light. Although getting the right qualifications was helpful, in a practical sense, contact with patients in later hospitals I worked in was far less direct and was marred by role and technique. It seemed wrong to relate to human distress in such artificial ways and various experiments with alternative modes of working followed. Antipsychiatry and phenomenological psychotherapy were by now my guiding lights, and the next logical step was to come to England, where all of this seemed so much further developed than in the South of France.

Living in one of the Arbours' therapeutic communities and working with the Crisis Centre provided the opportunity to examine my motivations and weed out some of my hypocrisies. Letting go of the comfort of a professional identity (together with a country and a language) meant touching rock bottom. Abandoning any remaining illusion of finding guidance in established theories, methods or individuals, freed me to trust myself at last and to start developing an approach which was in tune with what seemed important. The challenge was to be able to relate deeply and genuinely to the people I work with, without either getting drowned in their sorrows and distress or losing myself in the security of a pre-established framework. In the process of tackling it I have come across a number of people who have attempted to do just that, and most of them have been philosophers.

Theoretical Aspects

I have learnt much, first of all from Kierkegaard (1844, 1846), who represents to me the never-ending battle with existential anxiety. Reading him inevitably reminds me of the importance of starting from the core of insecurity in oneself, how crucial it is to keep discovering again and again that one is nothing, that there is a fundamental emptiness inside, that one is non-substantial and that nothing is ever given for keeps nor can be taken for granted—not one's possessions, not one's character, not one's achievements, or anything else in the world. The first step in any existential analysis must be to question all the layers of security around one and to find the empty space where one plunges into the precipice of one's own non-existence. Going back to this sense of *Angst*, or what Kierkegaard called this dizziness of freedom, brings home the realization that everything forever remains to be done anew and that the essence of being human is to not have an essence. Kierkegaard concludes from this that a new subjectivity and a new awareness are to be celebrated, rather than hiding in what others have prepared for you. You then become capable of standing up for the things you discover yourself. It is rather like learning to cook your own meal instead of going to McDonalds: finding the ingredients of life yourself and putting them together in a harmonious way. Kierkegaard also stresses how such a return to subjectivity coincides with the discovery of a new passion. It is inevitable that when one confronts the world from this position of vulnerability and with a willingness to fill the empty space with what is real to oneself, such anxiety, responsibility and truthfulness shine through as passion. When I become true to what really matters to me, I become passionate. I am no longer bored, because I no longer go along with what the crowd expects; I create my own meaning.

Nietzsche too went over this same ground—perhaps even in a more intense manner (Nietzsche 1878, 1881, 1882). While for Kierkegaard there is still a God in the background, who can provide a basic security, for Nietzsche the nihilistic position means that there is no longer a god to keep me safe. Now I have to do everything myself; I have to re-evaluate all the established values. I have to wonder why certain things are supposed to be right and others wrong; and then when I begin to set my own standards I have to question the world which I am thus creating myself. The locus of responsibility is shifted from "up there" to "in here". Everyone has to manage with their own conscience. There are no more parameters; there is no more framework. It is hardly surprising that Nietzsche went mad; it is all too easy to get lost in the chaos of existence when one is on one's own in a vacuum. Nietzsche's experience is invaluable in showing where the path of scepticism and subjectivity goes over the edge and becomes a recipe for disaster.

Fortunately, phenomenology (Husserl 1913, 1925) provides a method which makes sure that the enterprise of understanding existence has a less catastrophic outcome. Husserl's idea of the phenomenological reduction provides the systematic guideline to keep one on the right track. Maintaining the discipline of questioning one's assumptions leads one never to take the meaning of things for granted. Husserl showed the importance of suspending one's judgement and reaching for things as they directly reveal themselves. In this context he spoke of the need to "bracket" one's prejudice and assumptions about the world and deal with these separately, as one would when putting part of a mathematical calculation in brackets. The objective is to separate one's opinions from a pure description of what one observes. But such a description of phenomena in their outward appearance soon becomes an intuitive grasping of their deeper reality—as explanations are replaced with a search for direct contact and communication with what is there. The implications of this method for psychotherapy are tremendous, both in terms of putting one's therapeutic assumptions in brackets and in terms of seeing through clients' assumptions.

And so one arrives at the core of what all this is about together with Heidegger (1927, 1954), who more than any other philosopher pointed towards the miracle of being, to the wonder of all wonders: that there is in fact something rather than nothing. This is undoubtedly the essence of philosophy: to be in wonder and stop taking existence for granted. Assisting clients in rediscovering this source of life and curiosity underneath all the everyday complexities and complication must be one of the aims of existential analysis. The film *Wings of Desire*, by the director Wim Wenders, illustrates particularly well this touching upon and searching to grasp the wonder of being. Of course, Heidegger's other important contribution is that of rediscovering the crucial role of the human being in time. Again, this is about grasping that things are not given once and for all (as humans are sometimes inclined to pretend) but that we are in process, and are always "no longer" or "not yet". Such awareness of time as the essential element which defines us leads neither just to the reconsideration of one's past, nor simply to the need to think about one's future death; it shows up in every aspect of life as it is lived by me now. The reality of my failure at every minute to live up to my full potential of existence, the continuous process of dying in which I am engaged, is what also allows me to move forward and what makes it possible for me to face my destiny in a creative manner—with resolution, as Heidegger put it, or with the "courage to be", in Tillich's words (Tillich, 1952).

At the end of his career Heidegger, of course, found that resolution alone is not enough, is too one-sided. The humanists tend to ignore that insight as they insist on the importance of self-affirmation. Heidegger spoke of a double process, where resolution and releasement balance each other. A resolute and determined forward movement, facing existence's challenges, is now mellowed by the surrender to what is ultimately beyond one's ken and ability to comprehend. With an integration of apparent contradictions and a never-ending flow of becoming, a true existential dialectical process thus becomes possible.

In order to apply all this more concretely, some of Jaspers' ideas are invaluable (Jaspers, 1951, 1964). His notion of limit situations is particularly relevant to psychotherapy. It highlights the so easily forgotten fact that humans will inevitably come up against situations, experiences and events which will, as it were, cut them back down to size and put them back in their place as mere mortals. Death, chance, guilt and the uncertainty of the world imply that we will suffer sooner or later. This suffering and the poignancy of our limitations are what keeps us real and alive. When we try to deny our vulnerability and our fateful failure and helplessness, we block the process of transformation of which we are part. Awareness of these situations, together with wonder and doubt, is the beginning of our becoming ourselves. Paradoxically, people are inclined to hide and obscure these truths to themselves—and thus drift away from self-knowledge and into pathology.

Existential analysis, then, is about helping people to discover how they veil their awareness of those limitations and assisting them in the process of revelation of the underlying truth. This brings us back to Heidegger's notion of A-letheia, or truth, as that which is un-hidden. Sartre (1943a) too explored this avenue—and his descriptions of the ways in which people succeed in deceiving themselves are graphic, to the point and well-known. The whole concept of bad faith illustrates the pretence of claiming to have a substantial and secure being, which is expressed concretely in people's clinging to habits, fixed self-images and set roles and patterns of communication. The message is that this is all in vain, as our existence is neither fixed nor secure—and that coming to terms with this essential absence is ultimately the only way forward.

Another of Sartre's contributions (Sartre, 1939) is that of the idea of emotions and imagination as active instead of merely reactive, the notion that I can become aware of the way in which (as Heidegger put it) I am always attuned to the world in a certain way. Emotions are not some mysterious reactive phenomenon, but the culmination of a constant process of tuning into the world. My relation to the world is always coloured. I pick up and create atmospheres and moods. I focus on certain things and eliminate or ignore others. I attribute a certain meaning to the world, both cognitively and emotionally. If I allow myself to articulate these meanings to myself, I will learn much about my relationship to the world; I will understand something about my essential mode of being-in-the-world.

Methodological Aspects

It is self-evident that all of this is relevant to psychotherapeutic work. But when it comes to formulating more specific guidelines for the concrete practice of existential analysis, we have to turn to practitioners such as Binswanger (1946, 1963) and Boss (1957). I find that Gabriel Marcel's (1935) reference to the ideal of availability of the therapist is of central importance. For when he speaks of the need for a mutual readiness for what the future holds in store, he speaks of the therapist's willingness to be immersed in what the client is tackling—not just in an aloof, objective manner, but in such a way that it touches you, the therapist, directly.

Such a willingness to acknowledge the relevance of the client's struggles to one's own attitude towards life is the *sine qua non* of existential analysis. To recognize that we are all human, and that we are first and foremost united in this exposure to the human condition, sets the scene for a basically philosophical dialogue. I come to this dialogue with a fundamental openness to what human living and suffering entails—and with a readiness to find yet another new perspective on the same issues. Of course such resonance requires me to find myself stable enough and able enough to manage my own challenges and problems satisfactorily. Only then can I be available to further my understanding of the human predicament and my own struggles with it by exposing myself to confrontation with your particular viewpoint. I thus take your particular experience extremely seriously; I take it into myself and let it resonate with me. I allow myself to be transformed by our dialogue. Of course this is equally true for the client; the extent to which the client is truly available in the dialogue determines the measure of success of the psychotherapeutic process. But such an atmosphere of serious and open contemplation must in the first instance derive from the therapist's attitude. One cannot expect clients to lead the way.

Therefore, as I suggested before, neither can mere presence be sufficient. A simple "being-with" could easily lead to a morbid and melancholic going around in circles. The therapist needs to have more than mere empathy or sympathy. What is needed is a framework, a map which can provide some sense of where the client is struggling or trapped. This can also throw light on other parts of the territory of existence, and provide some perspective on what is currently experienced. Of course, such models can easily become restrictive instead of helpful, and it is important to stick to tentative sketches of the world and one's world-relation rather than be drawn into reductionistic models of the mind or the person.

Binswanger's notions of *Umwelt, Mitwelt* and *Eigenwelt*, as well as the implied *Überwelt* (van Deurzen-Smith, 1984), are useful in sketching the four dimensions of human relating to the world (see also Heidegger, 1954; Yalom, 1980). The fourfold complexity of natural or physical demands, social or public challenges, mental or private limitations, and the ultimate provocation by the unknown, can be seen as the background against which human paradoxes unfold. Figure 1 shows how contradictions are faced on each of these four levels and suggests likely points of stagnation, where only one side of the paradox is pursued.

Living means negotiating conflict, facing contradiction, tolerating paradox—we are always somewhere in between: no more and not yet, between birth and death, freedom and necessity, isolation and belonging, faith and doubt. Embracing life means daring to greet the inevitable suffering, anxiety and guilt as an intrinsic part of existence and as an opening up of our own horizons and possibilities.

Referring to a schematic map of human world relations, as in Figure 1, has the advantage of providing a representation of the fundamental boundaries of human existence and of clarifying the basic contradictions which are inevitably encountered in the different dimensions. With such a sketch of the territory of human existence in mind, it is sometimes easier to get a sense of where and how a specific conflict is situated. Of course, there is no suggestion of whether the pole of basic purpose or the pole of ultimate concern is more desirable. Human existence fluctuates between the high tide of fulfilment and the low tide of depletion, and neither one can be avoided or discarded without major unbalance and distress resulting.

Figure 2 illustrates the compass of the emotional cycle which may give a person a sense of where on life's territory he or she finds him or herself.

Dimensions of experience	Basic purpose	Intermediate goal	Ultimate concern
Natural world	Pleasure Vitality Strength	Health Comfort Wealth Fortune	Illness Weakness Misery Death
Public world	Success Power Glory	Recognition Fame Influence Respect	Failure Defeat Impotence Isolation
Private world	Integrity Selfhood Authenticity	Individuality Freedom Specialness Kinship	Disintegration Confusion Dissolution of self
Ideal world	Truth Ultimate reality Wisdom	Meaning Understanding Knowledge Faith	Absurdity Groundlessness Void

Figure 1 The territory of human experience. From van Deurzen-Smith, 1988

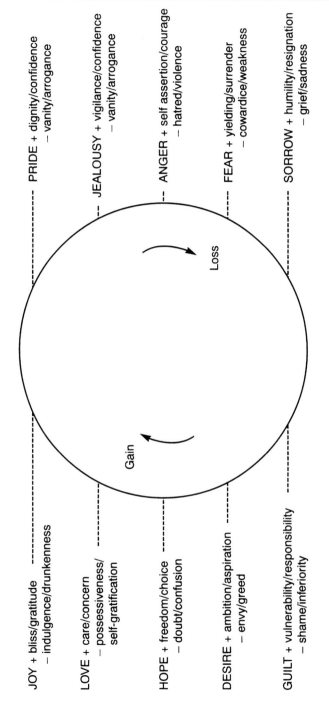

Figure 2 The compass of the emotional cycle. From van Deurzen-Smith (1988)

Emotions seen in this way, as indicators of meaning and direction, cease to be enemies or passive experience and become important existential realities instead. Each emotion or mood can now be savoured in its full intensity and appreciated for its dual positive and negative aspects. The aspiration or concern which is indicated by the emotion leads the way towards an exploration of the person's relationship to the world.

In undertaking such an exploration, the client works together with the existential analyst in a dialogue which investigates the client's interpretations of the world. It is the client's system of meaning which is to be clarified, without pressure from the analyst to conform to a previously established dogma or body of standard interpretations. What the analyst will constantly seek is the client's version of the truth.

Reaching for this truth is often guided by paying attention to existential anxiety and existential guilt (Boss, 1962; Yalom, 1980), which highlight the person's state of debt towards the world, others, self, and—more importantly—life.

In this way the focus of the analysis shifts from the explicit to the implicit. While always starting from the obvious, from what is actually there, the search is on to reveal the implied essence and meaning and to assist the client in a process of reconnecting with what is of true significance to her/him. Finding such significance requires a spirit of adventure and a readiness to face the full spectrum of challenges which human existence entails.

ILLUSTRATIONS OF EXISTENTIAL WORK

Marie-Louise: Letting Go of the Past in Order to Reclaim It

Marie-Louise is a 24-year old Frenchwoman. In the first interview she presents herself as a small but sturdy, colourfully dressed and generously made-up young lady. She works in England as an au pair and has done so for the last nine months. She left France because she did not know how to solve some of the situations she was involved in. She had broken off a three-year relationship with her boyfriend because he wanted her to marry him and move with him to another town, where he had just been offered a job. She felt this was a trap and that she would be unable to maintain her independence if she went along with him. Independence is one of the main values that Marie-Louise's choices are apparently based on. Of her three sisters (all older than her) two are married and installed in "bourgeois" family life. Marie-Louise has obvious contempt for this.

The third sister has an alternative life-style but is unable to manage her life satisfactorily. The parents are divorced after many years of fighting. Marie-Louise's picture of marriage is that of a battlefield where no one can win. Her picture of her own and her sister's alternative life-styles is that of a romantic voyage into nowhere.

She has fled to England to escape from the impossible choice between marrying her boyfriend and becoming like the two elder sisters and her mother, or opting for a bohemian life-style and ending up like her other sister. She now works for an upper-middle-class family in Richmond and spends all her time off with a group of free-floating people of her own age, around Hammersmith.

The problem she experiences is that of not knowing what to do with her life; every possible option seems to carry potential destruction. She thought she could solve things by starting a new life in England; now she realizes that everything is still the same, or worse. The French ex-fiancé has started a relationship with another woman. In the gang she hangs out with in England, there is a total denial of the value of a personal relationship. While she was pregnant, a few months ago, the other women in the group supported her in obtaining an abortion while using the occasion to cut her off from her privileged relationship with one of the men in the group.

They call her "Marylou" and do not seem interested in hearing about her past life in France. She is able to talk quite freely about her French life with Mildred, her employer, but she senses Mildred's pressure on her to conform and settle down in a "mature marriage". At this point in time there is no-one she trusts implicitly; everyone is out to make her give up something, and nobody really knows her. This theme recurs many times throughout the weekly therapy sessions that take place over a four-month period. Her trust in me is based chiefly on the fact that I at least admit what I want from her: a fee for the session and a commitment to working towards total frankness. What I offer in return seems most attractive to her: a joint building-up of an understanding of her experience in all its many facets and complexity; permission for her to explore the completeness of self that has been lost between her fear of being reduced to a conventional, "maturely" marrying, dependent Marie-Louise and a fear of being doomed to become Marylou, a desperately lonely outsider. We agree on a once-a-week arrangement, with a review after three months.

In the second session, Marie-Louise talks about a letter she has had from François, her ex-fiancé. He tries to make her feel jealous and offers her marriage again, more on his terms than ever. To Marylou it seems like a last chance to become "mature" and "dependent": if she refuses this time to go straight, she will have to be marginal ever after—that is how she views the dilemma. Most of the session is spent on exploring the definitions and fantasies that constitute the dilemma in her mind. What does it mean to be married? What does it mean to be marginal? What is her own world like inside, beyond those definitions of a way of life? What essential qualities of life are not to be found in either of those accounts of reality?

Slowly, Marie-Louise starts to talk about what life "should be like" or "could be like", instead of focusing on the two thus far impossible realities she has envisaged. It transpires that what matters most is to find a life where she will be with people who can listen to her and talk about those things that matter. She discovers that she wants: independence *and* romantic love, rather than either/or. We talk about her image of independence and dependence. She discovers that what she really values is autonomy, i.e. the ability to be a person in her own right, strong enough to remain true to herself while relating deeply to others.

Her Hammersmith group is, of course, in favour of "independence", but then it follows that love cannot exist: to maintain independence one has to reject commitment to anything or anybody. That is not what Marie-Louise wants, although it has often seemed the only way out of smothering relationships. She is starting to dis-identify with the ideas of Marylou. She is starting to identify her own personally meaningful ideas and aspirations. She is afraid it will not be realistic to live according to her own ideas, following her own conscience rather than the norm of some existing group in society; she does not think anyone will understand or agree.

She wonders where I will want to push her: will I stand by her when she makes her real self known, or will I come down in judgement, in favour of independence or dependence?

The next session, she challenges me. She breaks down in despair and cries for nearly half an hour uninterruptedly. There is no direct cause other than her expectation of me letting her down by trying to perk her up in spite of herself. She fears I may propose a solution, announcing my bias by choosing the "right life-style" for her. It is only because I do not do this and instead relate to her isolation and despair, to her fear, by letting her know that I respect it and will allow it, it is only because I show her this respect, first by saying these things and then by letting her cry her own sorrow through, that she starts to feel some confidence—not only in my understanding of her reality but mainly, and for the first time, in her own right to be just exactly the way she is.

The next session is different. Marie-Louise does not wear make-up any more: "It only messes up when I cry, anyways". She comes in to sort out her part in the relationship with François. She has still not replied to the letter he sent her two weeks ago; she is still overflowing with resentment for his treatment of her, his expectations of her fitting in with his life. I remind her several times of the importance of examining her active part in the relationship rather than focusing on her feelings about what he does to her. She discovers that by doing this she not only gets insight into her own character and actions, but also builds up a stronger image of herself as an active human being who does not exclusively respond, react and feel but also creates, initiates and acts.

This new way of viewing her relationship inspires her to write a letter to François the following week. She is pleased with herself for having formulated for the first time what she wants out of a relationship. She considers the relationship ended because she now knows what she does want to experience with a man.

During those weeks the sessions focus on her slowly building self-esteem. My interventions are all geared to help us to explore her inner frame of reference. The Catholic values are much more intrinsically present than she ever wanted to admit to herself. She is only able to claim her own rights once she has been able to acknowledge her own "guilt" in terms of the Catholic Church. Sleeping around and having an abortion are not things that she can easily forgive herself for; in order to live that life of "freedom" she has had to disown her conscience; she has had to live in "bad faith" with the created image of the independent Marylou. She has lost her substance in the process. Gradually, she is now rebuilding her own sense of worth and identity. Some time during these two months she receives a letter from Bernadette, her actress sister, who informs her of the attempted suicide of one of their mutual friends. Marie-

Louise understands that act as the only possible way out of the emptiness that follows the flight away from one's own inner reality. She is determined not to flee any more.

Following this decision she has several open disagreements with both her friends in Hammersmith and Mildred, her employer. She concludes that she cannot any longer "play the part" in either case. She decides towards the middle of the third month in therapy that the time has come for her to explore a more creative future; and she plans a trip to France to investigate training courses in social work. Her idea is to find a place in the world where she will be able finally to be herself and help other people to do so too.

She has now been in England for exactly a year and thinks she is ready to go back and face her sisters, her parents, even François if she happened to meet him. She is determined to stick to the values she has adopted as her own. To be autonomous rather than dependent or independent is the most crucial decision in terms of her relationship to her family. She fears, however, that no one will understand her new self, although she finds that Mildred has been more respectful of her since she applied for the social work courses and confronted her about the amount of work she was expected to do as an au pair.

We have already planned to have a last review session before her trip to France when she 'phones me in a panic one day. François has arrived in England without giving her any notice. He has come to see her in order to persuade her to come back and marry him. He affirms that he will respect her new sense of self, but he does not want to listen to her plans for study. Marie-Louise fears that her new autonomy will melt away in response to this new proposal, which for the first time includes her as a person important enough to make a trip to England and abandon his current girlfriend for. She is sure it will not last if she gives in now, but she is also sure, suddenly, that she loves him and wants him to love her. In that phone call, she decides to tell François all of this and then go off on the trip as planned, alone. The review session is spent considering her growing sense of direction in the midst of all the distractions and disappointments that she fears she will meet on her way. We discuss the middle way, between turning her back on people or situations because they have not allowed her to be herself or, on the other hand, merging into other people's opinions or ways of life giving up her inner reality. Marie-Louise decides that her commitment to a course of study is of essential importance to her because she needs time to establish her new reality more concretely and substantially. She still fears it will mean a choice away from the relationship with François. She leaves with doubts, anxiety and guilt about walking out on François a second time, albeit this time for positive reasons.

When she comes back to England a few weeks later, it is only to fetch her luggage and say her goodbyes to Richmond, Mildred, Hammersmith and me. We have two sessions during this time. Marie-Louise looks very different from the way she did four months ago: she has found her own image, somewhere between the classic woman and the rebellious teenager. She has obtained a place on the desired course, but is already disappointed with the curriculum. We examine her expectations and her attitudes towards the course. At the end, she seems clear enough about what it is she wants from the course without having to expect it to provide her with the ultimate answer.

We talk less about her parents and François than might have been useful. It would have been good to be able to have some more sessions now that a new way of life is being established. Marie-Louise herself is pleased she is leaving me behind in England. She wants to do it on her own now. She wants to have her disappointments and fears and live through them without assistance.

This seems a healthy attitude. Although I am aware of the limitations of the metamorphosis, a good deal seems to have been accomplished and I have a basic confidence in her positive attitude towards life, trusting that she will find her way.

A letter, 15 months later, indicates that Marie-Louise has had all the disappointments she expected. Her views on social work are certainly less idealistic than at the outset. She has, however, continued with her course of study and is finding satisfaction in her own ability to do so. She sees François at weekends and holidays, and there is a possibility of his obtaining a post near Marie-Louise's college. She says she would feel ready to live with him and commit herself to him if he were prepared to make his commitment clear by that move towards her.

It is very possible that the shortness and intensity of the therapy, combined with the urgency of the situation, was the crucial factor in making this case a successful one. Marie-Louise's motivation to sort out her life made it possible to focus on crucial existential issues and her strong desire to find her own way in the world made rapid transformation possible. The work she did demonstrates the relevance of the existential approach in dealing with crisis and life re-evaluation.

Vicky: Learning to Be More by Being Less

Vicky is a determined professional lady in her late 30s. She is referred by a colleague and makes contact in writing, presenting herself as "stuck at a number of crossroads in my life, carrying too much baggage to proceed and therefore in imperative need of personal therapy". At the initial interview she turns out to be of average height with short cropped ash-blond hair and small, expressive, metallic blue eyes. The overall effect of her appearance is the more striking as she is considerably overweight and dressed in colourful king-size dungarees. Although she gives the impression of being solidly self-confident, thick layers of masking cream barely hide severe acne. The cracks in this mask on her face seem to portray an inner turmoil and her vain attempts to cover it up. There is similarly an air of tiredness and defeat in the manner in which she sinks down to sit on the couch.

She says that she is a residential social worker, in charge of a large unit for severely emotionally disturbed children and that she generally enjoys her work. It is her sexuality and her marriage that are problematic. Although she and her husband Jim have a son (Mark), who is now seven years old, they have been unable to have another child, since she has had innumerable miscarriages. She is convinced that this has made her into a burden to her husband and she has given up hope that he is genuinely interested in her. She fears that she is nothing but an impediment to his freedom and therapy is meant to help her make up her mind about whether to remain with him or let him go. She is only fleetingly aware of the possibility that she is actually encouraging Jim to turn away from her. She knows that she has pushed him to go on a forthcoming trip to Canada by himself. He is half Canadian and has not been back to his home country for 15 years, but is to leave in a few weeks to go and stay with his Canadian family for two months. Vicky presents this as the inevitable crisis that will take him away from her forever. It is not clear whether she longs for him to leave and stay away, to leave and come back or to not leave at all. It is as if she has no confidence in her ability to love him, and be loved back. She almost hopes that he will stay away so that he won't have left because he wanted to but because she has sent him away. She speaks about all this very casually. Her suffering is only evident when she mentions their son Mark, who is trying hard to keep them together. She fears that Jim might persuade Mark to come and live with him in Canada if he really decides to settle there without her.

Most of the initial interview is spent on her descriptions of what she imagines Jim, Mark, her parents and her colleagues think of her. She is particularly preoccupied with her belief that she has deceived and disappointed Jim. She reckons that he was attracted to her because she seemed strong and nurturing, capable of taking care of him, whereas in fact she has turned out to be someone who forced him into marrying her because she got pregnant and who then slumped into illness and dependency following the miscarriages. She thinks that Jim must feel trapped and fed-up, and she feels she owes it to him to help him free himself from this unfair position that she has put him in. In all this she displays an extraordinary ability to remain in control of what she describes as a desperate situation. For someone who describes herself as dependent, she appears to be remarkably in charge of the destiny of the person she thinks she depends on. It is not surprising that she requests a short-term once-weekly therapy. We agree on a six-month working period, as this fits in with mutual schedules and commitments.

At the first session after this initial interview Vicky is much more concerned with her parents, and in particular with her father, than with Jim. Because her father is suddenly seriously ill in hospital after what should have been a routine operation, she is now very concerned with her own mortality and that of those whom she loves. I see my role at this stage as simply needing to point out the themes of inequality and unfairness. This is expressed, for instance, in her thinking it unfair that her father should be in worse health than her mother. He has always done the right things, like not drinking and smoking, whilst her mother has always pretty much done as she pleased and seems to fare much better than him physically. Also, later on in the session while she is talking about her father's affection for her, she remarks that she "just can't win". When I ask her what she means, Vicky explains that she thought she was pleasing her father by moving up the social ladder and by having been promoted to become Head of Unit. Then she discovered to her dismay that life once more was not fair, as her father seemed to indicate that he would have preferred her to be at home with her son and husband instead. She is prepared to dismiss the whole idea of not being able to win with stoicism, but when pressed to examine her view on what "winning" would consist of, she discovers that her whole attitude to life hinges on this—winning would mean living life on her own terms, doing everything she likes while still being liked and respected by everybody.

At first Vicky is rather casually dismissive about this and calls it her perfectionism. When asked equally casually, "and why not be a perfectionist?", she begins to investigate the contradictions inherent in her own attitude. Now the emphasis shifts from all this talk about other people and the outside world to her sadness about her mixed-up relationship with herself. Of course, she is nothing as simplistic as a perfectionist: her house is a mess that she wants to escape from, her body seems out of control, even her work-life takes up too much of her time. It is as if she is greedy for work, things, people, food and love, in a desperate attempt at getting a sense of fullness and worth. But once she has obtained what she was after, the fulfilment doesn't follow. So all her efforts seem in vain. No wonder she feels that life isn't fair.

The next week she speaks of wanting to be in the real world instead of in a fantasy world. When asked, she defines the real world as where she is in touch with other people, rather than where she constructs images that do not connect to anyone or anything else. When asked what is wrong with having a fantasy world, she launches into a long list of bad experiences in her childhood and adolescence. Each of these involved her expectations of other people being disappointed, sometimes violently so. Yet another theme also emerges—that of the discovery of her own power over others. She speaks of her memories of sexual play with her stepfather at the age of nine and ten. First she only sees this in the light of his abuse of her and her guilt feelings when he turned alcoholic some time after she had refused to carry on with the games. When I point out how she is implying having had quite a lot of influence on her stepfather, she remembers the sense of victory: the victory in the knowledge that he picked her and not her sister, victory also in that he gave her a valuable piece of jewellery one day and victory also in the sense of having had such an impact on him that he would need to turn to drink after she refused him. All this leaves her very thoughtful.

We are able to discover how this theme is repeated many times over in other relationships where she turns a sense of being abused into one of being in control and having mastery over others. The bitter after-taste in all this is that she can never believe that it is she who matters to people. She may have some power and influence, but always indirectly, for people do not choose her for what she is, but for what she does and provides. Her only consolation is that of having discovered in herself the strength to say "No" when she can't bear this any longer. In distilling the essence of this, we conclude that her relationships to other people seem to take place in a dimension of competition, where her only chance of winning is to take the upper hand, impressing people with her superior abilities (taking on lots of work, going out with lots of boyfriends in her teenage years, having lots of friends over to play with her son, eating lots of food to become huge and powerful). Of course, the only thing she really "wins" in this way is exhaustion and disappointment when people do not respond to this behaviour with the gratitude she would like them to display. She begins to realize that she actually alienates herself from any possible appreciation by others as, in effect, she casts them as opponents and even as the enemy.

At the third session this new understanding has translated into an image. She sees herself as stuck on a ridge on a mountainside overlooking the sea: she is comfortable and can see the whole world from up there, but she feels cold and isolated and is looking for a path down. She is aware of many ways in which she remains aloof from other people, including from Jim and Mark. Then she says: "I am often told that I should trust people more and believe they will like me". As this is said with scepticism, I respond by saying: "Why should you be so rash? What certainty do you have that they will like you? Why should they come to you on your ridge on the mountainside when you are the one who is not coming down?" This changes her rather flippant attitude suddenly into one of self-reflection as she realizes that she has not wanted to trust others. She takes a long time to respond and finally says with tears in her eyes and with the surprise of having made a new discovery: "Yes. I am really alone—I am the only one who can do it. I'm on my own". As it is near the end of the session, I merely reply: "Yes, and that's where I will have to leave you, it is time for us to stop". That moment carries a seriousness and understanding of being touched by the inevitability of human limitations. It carries her forward into a more certain direction, for she now realizes what she is up against.

During the fourth session, she is for the first time capable of exploring some of her strengths: she reports that she is a keen gardener and has her own allotment. Putting order into nature's growing process is a source of unlimited enjoyment for her, especially as she is good at it. The metaphor of this talent becomes a source of inspiration during future sessions. With some assistance, she learns to translate her difficulties at work, for instance, into terms of sowing and reaping, planting and weeding and pruning. This makes her see new possibilities in her work and gives her much courage for facing problems as if they were just part of the enjoyable activity of her gardening life. This gives her the concrete model she craved: life seems within her grasp. She knows she is good at gardening and she feels confident that she would know what to trim and cut and where to encourage flowering and blossoming. She glows with pride as she realizes that this turns everything that seemed like a bore, a duty and a danger into something that can only be a source of challenge and enjoyment. For the first time she sees her problems in perspective.

During the next few weeks a number of concrete events in her life provide plenty of challenges for her. Among other things, Jim has now gone to Canada and her mother has moved in with her. She easily loses sight of her gardening metaphor as the clouds gather and she feels threatened in many ways. During this time she explores other issues for which different understandings and metaphors are needed. One of the themes that now emerges is that of her fantasy of being self-sufficient. It is, of course, related both to her negative view of other people and to her joy in gardening. She has a longing to live in a small cottage on her allotment, surviving entirely within her own resources. As self-sufficiency is her ideal, one of the things she most despises is "middle-class women living off their husbands' salaries and prancing around to art classes". In exploring this statement it becomes clear that what she does not understand at all is why these women, whilst being totally dependent and in her opinion virtually useless, still expect to be loved and desired by their husbands. Vicky does not in the least expect to be loved, even though she thinks of herself as fairly deserving. So how can those women who don't do anything to deserve it expect to be loved; and what's more, how do they actually manage to be loved? It is clear now that in spite of her rejection of these women's behaviour Vicky actually envies the mysterious self-confidence and power over men that they seem to command.

She wonders why she cannot be loved in this way herself. I point out to her that she has forgotten that by climbing away, onto her mountain ridge in her aloof self-sufficiency, she is the one not available to others. She is the one not open for love. By denying her own need for others she is pushing others away. These contradictions in her own attitude are gradually becoming explicit in our dialogue together. She can grasp this in theory but it is harder to recognize her implicit rejection of others in practice. She often needs me to make her attitude explicit to her, so that she can recognize it, but even then it does not entirely connect to her inner desire to change. She is still reluctant to become fully aware of her way of being in the world.

This comes to the fore when Vicky begins to examine her relationship with her mother, who lives with her during this time. Both try to outdo each other in independence and self-sufficiency, whilst reproaching the other for not being more loving or needy. It seems extremely difficult for Vicky to let it sink in that to love means, among other things, to make oneself available and therefore vulnerable to needing the other. She has protected herself carefully from being hurt by others by pretending never to need anything from anyone. She does not, for instance, expect Jim to be faithful to her in Canada and has told him so in as many words before his departure. She makes it generally clear to him that she wants nothing from him at all, but is amazed that this pushes him away rather than bringing him closer. Each time I draw her attention to such contradictions in her attitude, she is surprised and somewhat relieved at rediscovering the hidden logic of the situation, which previously seemed strange and confusing. What used to seem unpredictable and unfair is beginning to make sense.

There are many complex past and present relationships that we can now examine in this light and Vicky is very astute in pointing out the patterns. Yet she remains blind to the contradictions of her own attitude in the present. She still prefers to believe that she really is open to others and does not like to think that this might be an illusion which allows her to maintain control whilst keeping others at a safe distance, which leaves her essentially lonely and cut off.

This paradox finally comes to a head in a real sense through an apparently unrelated event in her working life, which becomes a powerful vehicle for a new and deeply felt understanding. One day she arrives for therapy in a shocked and somewhat distraught state about something that has taken place at the week-end. The adolescents in her unit have been to a holiday camp with some of the staff for a week and on Saturday Vicky suddenly decided to pay them a surprise visit. Far from being rewarded for this generous extra bit of work, she has been fiercely disappointed upon finding the staff drunk, drugged and so much out of control of the children in their charge that they are thrown out of the resort the following day despite Vicky's intervention. Although she does not want to take official action against the staff, because it would have severe repercussions for them and for the establishment (and perhaps for her), she knows that her relationship with them will never be the same again. Her professional self-confidence is shocked to its very foundation.

When we calmly look together at the implications of this experience, we find that up to this point she has always been the popular, friendly colleague and superior. She takes great pride in being "one of the boys" with the mostly male staff. This time she has had to resort to authoritarian behaviour and has been mocked by them for being a spoil-sport. She is outraged and wonders if she has always been too gullible, not strict enough, too eager to please. Yet she is also profoundly hurt, especially for having been let down by a staff that she thought she could trust and for whom she has done so much. But in the end the most painful aspect of the experience is that they have called her "up-tight" and considered her to be on the other side of the divide: no longer "one of the boys". More than their reproaches, it is the realization that she herself is no longer able to condone such behaviour that shocks her. She is discovering with astonishment that the values that she thought she stood for have been replaced by a new set of values that she has not so far dared to make explicit to herself.

Our discussion brings out that she was always the sort of person who fought for freedom and against the establishment: she used to smoke dope and drink quite a lot herself and believed that experience to be part of the rights of the individual. She used to think of herself as something of a revolutionary and as an outright liberated and democratic sort of person. This was precisely why she used to hate her name: Victoria. It always seemed so out of keeping with what she believed in and wanted to be. And now suddenly, through this one event, she notices that for a long time she has lied to herself. She is really proud of her name and the values that it conjures up do not seem so terrible at all. When she sees that I do not condemn her for her hesitant reclaiming of old values, it is with some glee, as if in a long last homecoming, that she admits to secretly identifying with Queen Victoria and all she stands for, even though that is hard to acknowledge and goes against what she has long thought ought to be the case. While these things are clearly difficult to express, there is an obvious release of pent-up longing to be more true to herself, and with much sighing and wide-eyed tearfulness she finds relief in facing her new position in life.

It is now possible for us to see the past in a new light too. It has been such a struggle for her all those years to try and take everything in her stride and everyone under her wing. She has been so caught up in this one-sided attempt at being broad-minded and understanding that she is surprised at her own relief when her forced composure and unrealistic accepting attitude is broken. Floods of resentment and sadness come streaming out now that she lets down the barrier. Suddenly she can see all the contradictions in her attitude. Accepting everything that comes her way and bending over backwards to accommodate everybody's demands on her, but never daring to reject anything or anyone for fear of rejection, she has got herself into an untenable position. She can only keep on expanding and expanding without ever having the possibility of decompressing or eliminating. It is obvious that such one-sided behaviour can only lead to explosion.

The next few sessions are so many variations on this theme. Each elaboration of this small revelation of inner truth makes her understand herself a little better. Every week a little piece of the puzzle falls into place. Often she describes a situation that apparently has no relation to the puzzle until her attention is drawn to its relevance in terms of her basic choices and challenges. Then sometimes it clicks into place and the world makes a bit more sense. At other times she just needs to explore her experience, finding it too painful to consider the ways in which she limits herself by over-expanding herself. She goes through a phase where she loses her self-esteem when I challenge her rather too forcefully on the way in which she controls Jim by pretending to be all-accepting of him, while actually punishing him with further withdrawal and independence whenever he does something she inwardly disapproves of.

This clearly still is the blind spot in her understanding. It is almost impossible for her to notice the impact of her own withholding of demands. Although she recognizes the effect of her withdrawal from Jim when he becomes alienated from her, she finds it much harder to catch herself doing it, let alone stop doing it. She would love to be able to tell him that she needs his love so that he would not be pushed away, but she is not ready to even allow herself to fully experience that sense of need.

There are still too many deeply ingrained reasons for her wanting to maintain the independent, aloof and outwardly tolerant, but inwardly suffering and judgmental, attitude that keeps him away from her. She is actually deeply mistrustful of love altogether. She cannot imagine that she will ever be really loved.

Vicky still deeply believes that she cannot have any impact on others unless she puts up with everything they dish out to her. The fundamental purpose for her is to have an effect on and be in control of others. But this purpose is dressed up as an attitude of great acceptance and capacity to include anything and anyone. The straightforward making of demands and setting of boundaries that could lead to a positive control of her relationships to others is lacking: she does not dare to announce and affirm her exclusive rights and needs. When she is asked to muse over what it means to her to be exclusive, she discovers the entire concept to have long been taboo—exciting, but strictly taboo. Being selective and choosy is dangerous, for how can she know that what she will pick is right? Also, how can she continue to be acceptable to all if she is not accepting? When I point out to her that she is just as non-accepting and selective in excluding selectivity as an option she is shocked.

The idea that she may only have been fooling herself makes it easier to abandon her old ways. She begins to wonder about what it is she really wants out of life and other people, rather than continuing to assume that she already knows what she wants. This brings up many new aspects, new questions and issues that need exploring.

Around this time Vicky begins to take an active interest in undertaking various projects for her own enjoyment instead of for her professional ambition. She finds that she can use some of this ambition for personal purposes and use her energy to achieve joy for herself, instead of success at work which impresses nobody. Her priorities are gradually shifting. She is loosening her own expectations of herself and opening up to the terror and longing underneath.

When the sessions finish, after six months as planned, she evaluates her progress with great optimism. A follow-up session two months later shows that, although she is managing well, she is perhaps a little too keen on proving to herself and me that the therapy has been a success. It is clear that she is not always allowing her experience to touch her deeply and that she is still looking to outside achievements to fill up the inner longing. Perhaps the therapy should have continued longer to stabilize a new attitude of self-reflection and monitoring of experience. But, as Vicky herself puts it, there is enough for her to go on. Her attitude is constructive and confident. She will know where to find further assistance if and when she needs it.

Peter: Finding Oneself in Spite of Psychotherapy

Peter is a professional man of around 30. He is tall and thin and covers a basic shyness with a self-mocking attitude. As he speaks, he emerges as intelligent and highly articulate. He excels in verbal expression to such an extent that one would expect him to have cultivated his ability to a more academic level. From the start he relishes arguing with me, and yet most of what Peter says during our first meeting is tentative. He strikes me as a young man who knows that he has effectively played his way through life so far, but who has reluctantly realized that it is time to grow up.

There is a hint of defeatism in his voice, a suggestion of oppressive doubt. He is inclined to dismiss the therapeutic relationship out of hand as non-viable, yet there is also a curiosity and genuine vulnerability. I note that Peter would be unlikely to tolerate any directive attempts to control him. Existential therapy is therefore an appropriate choice, although I have some doubt whether he wants to be helped at all.

The main issue that he puts forward is that of his relationships. He has a girlfriend for whom he cares. Their relationship is long-standing, but it has been made difficult through his desire to be free and have other relationships. Now he has become aware of the hurt this has caused his girlfriend. He has somewhat reluctantly reached the conclusion that the relationship is worth committing to. His girlfriend wants to settle down and have children. He is not at all sure that he is ready for this.

He also feels incompetent at expressing his tender feelings, especially to his girlfriend, and he is worried about the times when he gets into a rage with her. He openly admits to having considerable misgivings about psychotherapy. He worries that it is self-indulgent. Peter cannot remember much about his childhood and does not think there is any point in trying to.

Hearing all of this I am aware of his status of reluctant client and I realize that working with him will be difficult. I suspect that short-term therapy appeals to him because it will allow him to get his feet wet and prove to himself and others that he can do this, without actually having to plunge in. We agree to a ten-week contract.

Peter misses the first session and at the second says that it is not very easy for him to concentrate because he keeps getting distracted by other ideas: everything leads to so many other avenues. Most of all he is afraid of confabulation. He might be pinning things down in one way when they were actually much more complex. It is always like this with him, he says: he always sees many aspects to things and this makes it difficult to take sides. He is afraid of committing some sort of injustice.

He says that while other people, for instance, tell loads of stories about their adolescence, he has none to tell. His preoccupation with getting things wrong and writing the story of his life in an unfaithful way is a serious one. The idea of being fair and just to reality as well as to other people emerges as a guiding principle for him. One could say this is one of his central values.

From here he moves on to contemplate the contradictions between his relationship to his girlfriend and the time he spends with his friends, smoking, drinking and arguing. He is dissatisfied with the long nights talking, for he always ends up worrying about the things he has said in anger, which leave him with an emotional hangover. I remark that smoking, drinking and arguing with his friends could be considered self-indulgences. He agrees and says that he believes that the time has come to commit himself to his girlfriend and that he has now decided to move in with her and away from the gang, who keep him within the old culture. He feels the need to assure me and him that this is for real. At the same time he is worried about what he might miss. We talk about his current way of life and he wonders why it is not satisfactory to him, even though it is easy. I suggest that much of what comes easily takes one on a downward spiral, which is ultimately self-destructive. He then contrasts it with the possibility of devoting oneself to a career, a relationship or even to raising children. I point out how these things involve effort rather than ease, but that they build something constructive in the process.

Peter is driven to question anything that reeks to him of "establishment" values and he talks of things turning around in vicious circles and not leading anywhere. "Don't they lead anywhere, are you sure?" I ask, and this makes Peter question whether it is of any use for things to lead somewhere. Every intervention I make evokes his counter-reaction. "Why", he says with a dismissive gesture, "should one build these things if life is meaningless anyway? Why should I bother?" "Maybe", I query back in return, "life only seems meaningless when one lives on the downward spiral in self-indulgence. Perhaps it becomes meaningful only when you put in the effort to build something up and move into an upward spiral".

The next session Peter arrives in a bad mood. Everything has gone wrong. He has had a row with his girlfriend. He has been rushing around doing various things that he describes, and each in turn has led him to losing his temper with people and then getting worried about what they will think of him. He tells me how he used to have a real temper problem until he decided at some point in his early 20s that he should not lose his temper so often. Lately, however, he has begun to fear that suppressing the anger might be bad for him and he lets his temper flare up again now. He goes off into generalizations and after a minute I stop him and ask him to recount the concrete events that triggered his anger.

He tells me of his frustration with his girlfriend, who, after having a good time out with her own friends, overwhelmed him with her stories about it and then resented him not going to bed at the same time as her, because he wanted to write. When he finally did go to bed, she woke up, "only to have the last word". The next day, when she stopped him again when he was writing, he shouted at her that she was not respecting his needs.

We talk about what is required when two people have just moved in together and need to find ways to accommodate each other. Peter concludes abruptly that the cause of all the trouble is his busy social life. He decides to withdraw from these social relationships completely. He looks wounded and martyred as he makes this announcement and I inquire what that decision will do to him. He admits that no social relationships will mean boredom. I point out how the extreme positions of total immersion in these social relationships on the one hand or total withdrawal from them on the other hand both seem unsatisfactory. It sounds as if there must be a better solution somewhere nearer the middle of that continuum. It would be important to understand what these relationships offer him. Peter then begins to consider what they actually involve and he describes how he tends to use them for getting into arguments over trivia. It is as if he picks fights to prove himself worthy. I note that it looks as if he seeks to test his intelligence, but does this in a way that seems wasteful.

Peter is despondent and fears he is going around in circles again. I suggest that the trick is to find a way to make these circles turn into upward spirals instead of downward ones.

A week later Peter is looking relaxed when he comes in and says that things have been better. He has not gone out so much and has worked hard and is getting some results. This is largely because he had deadlines to meet. Later on, it transpires that he does the same thing in many different guises: using other people's deadlines or commitments as parameters for his own activity. He is, for instance, getting his girlfriend to persuade him to have children. I remark how he seems to be waiting for other people to push him into action, whilst keeping himself smugly at a distance from the decision-making.

Peter responds strongly to my use of the word "smug". Other people have called him smug and he does not like it. He thinks it is a bad thing to be smug and asks me if I think it is a bad thing. He suddenly sounds small and dependent, wanting guidance. We begin to examine what smugness means to him and how it might apply to him. Yes, he does have a basic ease with life and a sense of having sorted things quite nicely. He does not really want to look into himself and because he avoids doing so, he has not discovered what is inside him. I say: "You have not really been broken by life, you have not ever been truly challenged and in a way you long for it and in another way you want to keep things as they are". He says he has never even been to a funeral. He has never had his heart broken. I say: "You have never suffered real loss and it is through loss that people get most challenged, is it?"

He is not sure, but he wants to know how he can find something that will challenge him. He says he worries that he is too egotistical. He starts arguments for the sake of the argument and for his own pleasure. He pushes people until they give in or give up. "So you always win?" "Yes", he says, self-satisfied and embarrassed at the same time. "It sounds as if you are arguing with the wrong people, then—you have not met your match." This strikes another chord. He has apparently become so confident that he argues on other people's points, rather than pursuing his own line of thinking. He does not believe strongly enough in anything to want to argue it for its own sake. It is as if he has become bored with arguing itself for lack of commitment. "You don't let yourself be challenged and stretched there either", I comment. He sighs and talks about how he sometimes wonders about taking up some strict discipline, like Islam. Fundamentalism has a fascination for him, because of his yearning for boundaries and rules: his longing for something to come up against, be challenged by. He yearns for something greater than himself that will both stretch him and provide him with an outside parameter to grow up against, or towards. I note that it is not so much a boundary as a goal that he lacks.

At one point he says that our work together has given him plenty of new retorts for arguments, although he has not found opportunities to apply them. I feel under pressure to match him and stretch him, but also to spare him and leave him the illusion that he can win. It would be all right if he were fighting his hardest, but Peter seems to play in a noncommittal manner. It is as if he fears that if he commits himself to something he might lose. He is not prepared to really hazard himself, but this withdrawal dissatisfies him as much as it does me.

I confront him with this, saying how he seems to use all his energy and considerable abilities to play around instead of getting on with life. I am now convinced that he has taken the therapy in the same way as he takes life: passively, and seeing it as something he wants to win, but without wanting to put in the labour that is required or take a risk.

I put it to him at the end of the session that underneath his smugness he has a sense of falling short and of wasting his abilities. He sits up and takes notice, there is a sense of poignancy. Then Peter claims to have little or no ambition and a very unclear sense of his own possible contribution in life. Although I can challenge his smugness, I cannot provide anything to fill the emptiness with until he has learnt his own lessons through an actual experience of loss and subsequent discovery of what matters to him.

At the next session there is a long silence to start with. At last he hesitantly ventures: "I am not sure I want to be thinking about the meaning of life. I work all week and this hour is the most demanding of the week. I don't know that I want to be making this effort. There is nothing really wrong with my life. I am making changes anyway. I used to be into short-term happiness of the moment and that seems to be fading, but it is too much of an effort to plan anything else".

He speaks of his work, sitting at the computer and knowing that he is not producing things that are as good as he is capable of producing. He knows he could do better, but he doesn't. I remark that he sounds like a school teacher giving himself a bad report. He says that is frequently what teachers used to say about him and it is true. He knows that he can do better, but it just doesn't seem worth the effort.

I point out how sceptical he seems to be of almost everything that might be of value. "I am cynical", he says. "Yes, and proud of it", I reply. He blushes and grins. He asks me if it is wrong to be cynical and if he should change. I tell him I don't think that is the relevant question as long as he clearly does not want to change. I also note that someone who has a lively mind and who is used to questioning things cannot just stop doing so.

After a further exchange I say: "It seems to me that it all depends on how you use that ability to question, whether you use it to take you forward or whether you let it get you stuck". He is not quite sure he understands this. I give the example of someone who questions that two and two equals four. I say that such questioning might lead you to discover new mathematical principles if you acted on your scepticism and moved into some new form of mathematical investigation. However, if you did not act on your scepticism in order to discover some new truth, if instead you merely continued to question that two and two is four, without any further action, then you would in effect be stopping both your own progress and your ability to ever make any useful ordinary calculations in your life. Scepticism is only the first step. If you don't move beyond it, it might cripple you rather than serve you. I add: "In your case, your cynicism may be an essential asset if you know what to do with it, but right now it looks like it often stops you from engaging with life".

He is quiet for a while. Then he says, almost to himself: "I think I may have a problem after all—for nothing really seems meaningful or possible to me. There is no purpose, not even looking for a purpose seems meaningful". I remain quiet. The silence seems to weigh on him. "It is so intense here", he complains and he looks pained. "Life just does not seem meaningful. It is not perfectible, only manageable". "And sometimes not even that", I add. He immediately bounces back. "I have never felt I could not manage", he says confidently and with some surprise at his own certainty on this point. I say: "Yes, your issue is not that you are stressed or distressed, but rather under-stressed: there is not enough creative tension. You have found a great way of keeping tension at bay". He agrees and instantly reverts back to blaming this on his laziness. I point out how dismissive it is to brush off a coping strategy as mere laziness. He says that he has accepted that life does not bring happiness or satisfaction since he was in his early 20s. I see him suppressing a sigh. I ask: "What were the dreams you abandoned?" He moves into dismissive style: "O, I sang and I wrote, but I could never achieve that perfection, that bliss, that you sometimes, rarely, feel when you listen to certain music or read a novel. Take Nabokov, for instance. He brings together so much detail: it is like seeing all the knots—then he flips it over and suddenly you are faced with the perfection of a well knotted carpet. Sometimes in a film as well, you feel so transported, it is bliss, but it is short-lived. I've accepted that I can't share that with people. I've tried maybe once or twice, when I was drunk, but they can't understand". He has suddenly come to life as he momentarily allows himself to resonate with this dimension of deep yearning inside of him. He is poised to dismiss it.

I gently remark how he cuts himself off—from others, from his aspirations, from his own future, from his ability to create such moments. He protests that that is not his doing, but life. He says life is basically pretty meaningless. I say, "Yes, to those who expect it to carry intrinsic meaning". "Maybe I am just more passive than active", he ponders mournfully. Then he asks me whether I think that he would get meaning out of having children. I point out to him how he reverts to asking me to give him guidance instead of following his own. He contends that it makes no difference if life is intrinsically meaningless anyway. "That is the way of talking of someone who doesn't see meaning in life. You conclude that there can't be any meaning, because it is not there intrinsically. You are ruling out the possibility that if there is no meaning to start with, it is up to you to create some, like Nabokov creates carpet magic".

Peter looks puzzled. He says he does not understand. I sense that he is on the verge of discovering his own power to create, works of art in his job, constructive relationships and possibly children. The creativity is within his grasp and he knows it on some level, but he has made it taboo for himself and I sense that he wants me to guide him towards it so that he can discard and dismiss it again. I realize that he will have to understand why he has made his creative power so taboo before he can reach out for it again. I do not think he is willing or able to do so through my intervention.

Peter comes to the next session in a rebellious mood. He announces that he has moved and then maintains a heavy silence which I allow to unfold. He tells me that there are three things that bothered him in the last session. The first is that he is cynical, the second that he cuts himself off emotionally and the third that he makes me feel as if he is asking me to give him guidance. He also realizes that all three are connected. The first two things he can accept, but it really bothers him that I think that he wants guidance. His cynicism wouldn't even let him, he explains, for how can you ever tell anyone how to live their life?

I point out to him that far from thinking that he wants advice in order to act on it, I have the impression that he wants me to give him guidance so that he can reject it. In the same way in which he keeps his past out of his field of vision, he is also good at keeping others at a safe fighting distance.

He rises to my implied challenge by saying that there is nothing worth going over in his past and that he has learned not to show his emotions, living in the East End. In the working-class atmosphere in which he grew up, you just had to keep yourself from others emotionally and not give anything away. "What's the point in saying I have had a difficult childhood and that that is why I am who I am?" he says, rather scornfully. Then he goes on to recount a number of events in his past that throw new light on the way in which he conducts himself. He realizes that his memories are there to be retrieved if he wants to. He can also see that most of what he talks about today is full of sadness and resentment.

I wonder if he will have the courage to take the work a stage further, but as it happens he goes off on a two-week holiday with a group of friends at this point. Upon his return it is clear that he has withdrawn from the work that we have begun. He is more cynical and aloof than before and I wonder why he bothers to continue to see me. As soon as we get anywhere near serious he reverts to scepticism or mockery. I observe how it seems as if he runs into the sea, dips his toes in, then sees the waves and runs back. He does not plunge in and he does not try to swim. I decide to pressure him less and my interventions become more succinct and are often paradoxical in nature. If he asks, "How can I be more self-reflective?" I reply, "Why should you want to be?" When he talks of being lazy, I retort "Why not be lazy?".

This works well to a certain extent, for it fires him into showing his potential for creativity. Peter is definitely at his best when challenged to deploy his strength. In the end, however, he tends to disengage from the exchange, determined to stay in control of his own destiny, afraid to respond positively to external influences. A pattern develops, whereby he starts out with a half-hearted effort to work on something, then rises to the challenge that I offer, taking a considerable step forward, only to take two steps back a little later, undoing anything that could be seen as having come from me.

When we come to the end of our contract and it is time to evaluate our work together, I suggest that he is good at actively protecting his own living space but that he pays an important price of lack of stimulation, challenge and creativity for that. He has kept me out successfully, in the same way in which he keeps others at bay. He does not let his past or his future impinge on the present. I contend that the way in which he treats the therapy says a lot about his attitude towards life. "Yes, how do I do that?" He sounds anxious. "You can blame it on me if you want to", I suggest, half jokingly.

For the first time in our work together, he is the one who insists on being serious. "I don't want to blame it on you", he says. "How do I run away from therapy?" he insists. "You flee by withdrawing into cynicism or into abstractions. You keep things on a narrow base by not bringing things like dreams, memories, fantasies, and rarely even real events, concrete interactions, feelings, preoccupations. You keep things on an even keel by going over well-rehearsed arguments, keeping me out of your internal life and proving me wrong all the time. You have rarely talked about your parents, or your sisters and brother, or concrete things that happen between you and others. You have never even mentioned your girlfriend's name". There is a thoughtful silence. He avoids my eyes. Then he lifts his head and says: "I would like to try". At that moment the clock that indicates that our time is up begins to strike. "Saved by the bell, Peter", I say. He gets up slowly. The next session will be the last.

In the last session he again brings me the issue of not being able to concentrate. He tells me that it is related to him having had to learn to skim-read for his job. "Ah", I say, "This is wonderful. You have just summed up in one image the pattern that you have been struggling to describe and understand for the past months. It is a pattern that we have seen at play in many different aspects of your life, including in the way you have approached therapy. There are too many books, too many friends, too many possibilities, too many avenues to quickly explore, resulting in a lack of depth and purpose. But not only do you show how it is that you operate in those moments: skimming the surface and gathering quantity rather than quality, you also tell me why you do it. It is possible for you to do this, you say, because you have taught yourself to do so for practical purposes. You need to get through a lot and fast. So you have adapted and learned to do it".

He beams, but states dismissively: "Well, that is what comes easy to a lazy person". He is persistent and determined in holding on to this negative self-image. I am not playing ball. "Nah", I say, "That is a very personal view of the matter. What you refer to as the easy result of laziness would seem like something quite difficult to achieve to some other people. You find it easy to spread yourself thinly and skim the surface, whilst there are others who have the greatest difficulty in emerging from self-absorbed depth. Some people find it hard to even get through one book, for instance, let alone skim-read so many.' He accepts the credit for this particular talent.

After some further discussion Peter begins to wonder whether he might also be capable of a more profound approach at times. "You think that I have that in me?" he asks. "I know that you have that in you from the evidence you have given me over the past weeks and months." "How do I bring that out?" he asks, and I reply that life will do that sooner or later, if he is willing to learn from what happens to him. Now he moves on to wondering why life has spared him so much to date. We have been there before, but he is now able to find some answers for himself. He comes to the conclusion that it is two-sided. In the first place, he has been spared major tragedies up to now, but in the second place, when difficulties have hit him he has been able to keep them under control. He acknowledges both his ability to keep things safe and avoid trouble in that way and the risk of losing out on letting himself be touched by life.

I reflect on the ten sessions we have had, saying that these too seemed for him a time to try to get through relatively unscathed and that he did so successfully. He remarks, tongue in cheek, that he came to me with honorable intentions but that he will walk away from these sessions to go right back to where he was, untouched. "And that was just the point you wanted to prove", I reply, "that you could do that and that you were emotionally independent". "Yes, in a way, but that would be just what you would say". "Not necessarily", I reply, "there are other possible interpretations. For instance, that you feel like a failure for not having been able to get more deeply involved". He nods. "Or that you had to postpone it, so that you could come to the end and recognize that all the work in a way is yet to be done, so that these ten sessions were just a way to test the ground so that you could start proper therapy after that". "I have wondered about that", he says, "you think I ought to do that?" "Not until you feel ready for it", I reply.

I am not surprised when Peter responds to a very detailed written account of our work together with comments that are thoughtful but largely dismissive. His tone is jokey and sometimes sarcastic. Although it hurts to see my work rejected in this way, I recognize that Peter is confirming his ability to be in control of his own life and his therapy, claiming his right to not be reduced to the status of client. It would be easy to pathologize Peter and to see his response as evidence of a deep-seated problem for which he urgently requires more therapy.

Nothing would be gained from such an approach and I prefer to respect Peter's determination to protect his independence of thinking about himself and to confirm his ability to emerge victorious from what could have been a fairly threatening situation. That is the gain from therapy that he claimed for himself, to some extent at my expense. It is not what I would have planned for him or what gratifies me the most, but it is not for me to plan my clients' learning and my gratification comes from being able to do a professional job with integrity.

I am convinced that life will confront Peter with his refusal to learn from others until he eventually finds a way to do so. It was not within my gift to teach him that in ten sessions. It remains noteworthy that Peter made some significant changes in his life at the same time and very much despite his work with me. This indicates that his commitment to improving himself is real and that he needs to do it under his own steam and in his own time. I would conclude that he has ample personal resources to draw on and that our work together played some small part in focusing his considerable strengths, paradoxically by bringing into awareness some of his current limitations in using them.

5

CONCLUSION

Throughout this book, examples have been given of ways in which the human condition confronts people with situations that lead to suffering and to having to cope with ambiguity. It is up to us whether we let such intensity result in nothing but pain, or whether we find ways to enhance our appreciation and joy in the miracles that life can also deliver to us. It depends to a large extent on our own attitude whether we let adverse circumstances bring us down and lead us into the impasse of meaninglessness, or whether we rise to the challenge and turn crises into opportunities.

The paradox of life is that we need challenges in order to be woken up from our inertia and brought back to reality, whereas a smooth and easy life leads us to complacency. At the same time, it is entirely human for us to seek the easy way. Most of us have a fundamental inclination to opt for those things that will stop us from coming to life or learning. This means that there is always the risk of us becoming more dead than alive, losing out on the passion that enhances our everyday experience. Boredom and emptiness may therefore be enemies as great as trauma and crisis.

It is ultimately always possible to find new sources of passion. The most desperate situations still procure opportunities. Valuable lessons of life can be learnt from the very challenges that we desperately try to avoid. It is always possible to reconsider a particular life event and find a new significance and meaning in it. Existential psychotherapy encourages people to do just that: to prize and relish their small and large agonies and to learn to live bravely through their life's trials and tribulations. The objective then becomes not to escape from difficulties but to face them, not to blame oneself, or others, or life itself for what is hard and impossible, but to try and understand it and take it into one's stride.

It should be evident from the previous pages that paradox and passion are just as important in the client's life, in the psychotherapist's personal experience and in the therapeutic process. There are no short cuts for understanding other people: we have to take the long and confusing way through our own experiences of pain and failure. We have to allow ourselves and our clients to be exposed and in danger at times and we also have to know how to make ourselves and our clients safe again. This requires us to be moved by passion and yet to be steady and purposeful in our progress through the maze of life. It is only as we struggle with our paradoxes and dilemmas that we can gain such steadiness with the necessary clarity of mind.

REFERENCES

Andersen, H.C. (1835). The Little Mermaid. In Andersen, H.C., *Fairy Tales and Legends*. London: Bodley Head, 1935 edn.

Barnes, M. and Berke, J. (1973). *Mary Barnes: Two Accounts of a Journey Through Madness*. Harmondsworth: Penguin.

Barrett, W. (1986). *Death of the Soul*. Oxford: Oxford University Press.

Baudrillard, J. (1986). Forgetting Baudrillard. *Social Text*, **15**, 140–44.

Baumeister, R.F. (1991). *Meanings of Life*. London: Guilford.

Berdyaev, N. (1948). *The Destiny of Man* (transl. Duddington, N.). London: Geoffrey Bles.

Bettelheim, B. (1987). *A Good Enough Parent*. London: Thames and Hudson.

Binswanger, L. (1946). The Existential Analysis school of thought. In May, R., Angel, E. and Ellenberger, H.F. (eds), *Existence*. New York: Basic Books, 1958 edn.

Binswanger, L. (1963). *Being-in-the-World* (transl. Needleman, J.) New York: Basic Books.

Boss, M. (1957). *Psychoanalysis and Daseinsanalysis* (transl. Lefebre, J.B.). New York: Basic Books.

Boss, M. (1962). Anxiety, guilt and psychotherapeutic liberation. *Review of Existential Psychology and Psychiatry*, **11**(3), September.

Bowlby, J. (1979). Psycho-analysis as art and science. *International Review of Psycho-Analysis*, **6**, 3–14.

Brown, D.E. (1991). *Human Universals*. New York: McGraw-Hill.

Buber, M. (1923). *I and Thou* (transl. Kaufman, W.). Edinburgh: T&T Clark, 1970 edn.

Buber, M. (1929). *Between Man and Man* (transl. Smith, R.G.). London: Kegan Paul, 1947 edn.

Buckingham, L. (1992). A headache that just won't go. *The Guardian*, 31 October, p. 38.

Camus, A. (1942). *The Myth of Sisyphus*. Harmondsworth: Penguin, 1975 edn.

Collingwood, R.G. (1958). *The Principles of Art*. Oxford: Oxford University Press.

Cooper, D. (1967). *Psychiatry and Anti-psychiatry*. New York: Barnes and Noble.

Dante, A. (1307). *Divine Comedy*. Harmondsworth: Penguin.

Dennett D. (1991). *Consciousness Explained*. London: Penguin.

Derrida, J. (1979). *Spurs: Nietzsche's Styles*. Chicago: University of Chicago Press.

Eliot, G. (1872). *Middlemarch*. Harmondsworth: Penguin, 1994 edn.

Eliot, T.S. (1930). Ash Wednesday. In *Selected Poems*. London: Faber and Faber, 1954 edn.

Eliot, T.S. (1944a). Little Gidding. In *Four Quartets*. London: Faber and Faber.

Elliot, T.S. (1944b). Burnt Norton. In *Four Quartets*. London: Faber and Faber.

Fairbairn, W.R.D. (1952). *An Object-relations Theory of the Personality*. New York: Basic Books.

Federn, P. (1953). *Ego Psychology and the Psychoses*. London: Maresfield.

Foucault, M. (1961). *Madness and Civilization* (transl. Howard, R.) London: Tavistock, 1967 edn.

Foucault, M. (1969). *The Archeology of Knowledge* (transl. Sheridan, A.). London: Tavistock, 1972 edn.

Frankl, V.E. (1946). *Man's Search for Meaning*. London: Hodder and Stoughton, 1964 edn.

Freud, S. and Breuer, J. (1895). Studies on Hysteria, *Standard Edition*, Vol. II. London: Hogarth.

Hartmann, H. (1956). The development of the ego concept in Freud's work. *Essays on Ego Psychology*. New York: International Universities Press, 1964 edn.

Heaton, J. (1997), Existential psychotherapy. In Feltham, C. (ed.), *Which Psychotherapy?* London: Sage.

Heidegger, M. (1927). *Being and Time* (transl. Macquarrie, J. and Robinson, E.S.) London: Harper and Row, 1962 edn.

Heidegger, M. (1954). *What Is Called Thinking?* (transl. Scanlon J.) The Hague: Martinus Nijhoff, 1977 edn.

Hume, D. (1739). *Treatise on Human Nature*. London: John Noon.

Husserl, E. (1913). *Ideas* (transl. Boyce Gibson, W.R.). New York: Macmillan, 1931 edn.

Husserl, E. (1925). *Phenomenological Psychology* (transl. Scanlon, J.). The Hague: Martinus Nijhoff, 1977 edn.

Jacobson, E. (1964). *The Self and the Object World*. New York: International Universities Press.

Jaspers, K. (1951). *The Way to Wisdom* (transl. Manheim, R.). New Haven, CT: Yale University Press.

Jaspers, K. (1964). *The Nature of Psychotherapy*. Chicago: University of Chicago Press.

Jones, E. (1953). *The Life and Work of Sigmund Freud*, Vol. 1. New York: Basic Books.

Kernberg, O. (1980). *Internal World and External Reality*. New York: Jason Aronson.

Kierkegaard, S. (1844). *The Concept of Anxiety* (transl. Thomte, R.) Princeton: Princeton University Press, 1980 edn.

Kierkegaard, S. (1846). *Concluding Unscientific Postscript* (transl. Swenson, D.F. and Lowrie, W.). Princeton: Princeton University Press, 1941 edn.

Kierkegaard, S. (1855). *The Sickness unto Death* (trans. Lowrie, W.) Princeton: Princeton University Press, 1941 edn.

Kierkegaard, S. (1844). *The Concept of Dread* (transl. Lowrie, W.). Princeton: Princeton University Press, 1944 edn.

Kohut, H. (1972). Discussion of Ernest S. Wolf, John E. Gedo and David M. Terman's paper: "On the adolescent process as a transformation of the self". In *The Search for the Self*, Vol. II. New York: International University Press, 1978 edn.

Laing, R.D. (1967). *The Politics of Experience*. London: Tavistock.

Laing, R.D. (1959) *The Divided Self*. Harmondsworth: Penguin.

Laing, R.D. (1961). *Self and Others*. Harmondsworth: Penguin.

Laing, R.D. and Esterson, A. (1964). *Sanity, Madness and the Family*. Harmondsworth: Penguin.

Laing, R.D. (1985). *Wisdom, Madness and Folly*. London: Macmillan.

Lasch, C. (1984). *The Minimal Self: Psychic Survival in Troubled Times*. London: Pan.

MacNeice, L. (1949). *Selected Poems of Louis MacNeice*. London: Faber and Faber, 1964 edn.

Marcel, G. (1935). *Being and Having: An Existentialist Diary*. New York: Harper and Row, 1965 edn.

Miller, A. (1979). *The Drama of the Gifted Child*. London: Faber and Faber.

Nietzsche, F. (1883). *Thus Spoke Zatathustra* (transl. Hollingdale, R.J.). Harmondsworth: Penguin, 1961 edn.

Nietzsche, F. (1886). *Beyond Good and Evil*. New York: Vintage, 1966 edn.

Nietzsche, F. (1887). *On the Genealogy of Morals* (transl. Kaufman, W. and Hollingdale, R.Z.) New York: Vintage Books, 1969 edn.

Nietzsche F. (1889). *Twilight of the Idols* (transl. Hollingdale, R.J.). Harmondsworth: Penguin, 1969 edn.

Nietzsche, F. (1878). *Human, All Too Human: A Book for Free Spirits*, (transl. Hollingdale, R.J.) Cambridge: Cambridge University Press, 19   edn.

Nietzsche, F. (1881). *Daybreak: Thoughts on the Prejudices of Morality* (transl. Hollingdale, R.J.). Cambridge: Cambridge University Press, 1987 edn.

Nietzsche, F. (1882). *The Gay Science* (transl. Kaufman, W.). New York: Vintage Books, 1974 edn.

Nussbaum, M.C. (1994). *The Therapy of Desire: Theory and Practice in Hellenistic Ethics*. Princeton: Princeton University Press.

O'Hara, M. (1986). Heuristic inquiry as psychotherapy: the client-centred approach. *Person-Centred Review*, **1**(2), 172–184.

Pascal, B. (1662). *Pensées*. Paris: Gallimard, 1962 edn.

Plato. *Portrait of Socrates*. London, Oxford Press, 1938 edn.

Plato. *The Republic*. Harmondsworth: Penguin, 1955.

Pope, A. (1963). Moral Essays. In Butt, J., *Poems by Alexander Pope*. Newhaven, CT: Yale University Press.

Popper, K. (1962). *Conjectures and Refutations*. London: Routledge and Kegan Paul.

Read, H. (1946). *Collected Poems*. London: Faber and Faber.

Rieff, P. (1966). *The Triumph of the Therapeutic*. Harmondsworth: Penguin.

Sartre, J.P. (1943a), *Being and Nothingness: An Essay on Phenomenological Ontology* (transl. Barnes, H.). New York: Philosophical Library, 1956, edn.

Sartre, J.P. (1948). *Anti-Semite and Jew*. New York: Shocken Books.

Sartre, J.P. (1939). *Sketch for a Theory of the Emotions*. London: Methuen, 1962.

Sartre, J.P. (1943b). *No Exit* (transl. Gilbert, S.). New York: Knopf, 1947 edn.

Shapiro, D.A., Firth-Cozens, J. and Stiles, W.B. (1989). The question of the therapist's differential effectiveness: a Sheffield Psychotherapy Project Addendum. *British Journal of Psychiatry*, **154**, 383–5.

Smith, S. (1983), *Stevie Smith, A Selection*. London: Faber and Faber.

Spence, D. (1982). *Narrative Truth and Historical Truth: Meaning and Interpretation in Psychoanalysis*. New York: W.W. Norton.

Spinelli, E. (1989). *The Interpreted World: An Introduction to Phenomenological Psychology*. London: Sage.

Tillich, P. (1952). *The Courage to Be*. Newhaven, CT: Yale University Press.

Tillich, P. (1954). *Love, Power and Justice*. Oxford: Oxford University Press.

Truax, C.B. and Mitchell, K.M. (1971). Research on certain therapist interpersonal skills in relation to process and outcome. In Bergin, A.E. and Garfield, S.L. (eds), *Handbook of Psychotherapy and Behavior Change: An Empirical Analysis*. New York: Wiley.

Truax, C.R. (1963). Effective ingredients in psychotherapy: an approach to unravelling the patient–therapist interactions. *Journal of Consulting Psychology*, **10**, 256–63.

van Deurzen-Smith, E. (1994). *Can Counselling Help?* Durham: Durham University Publications.

van Deurzen-Smith, E. (1995). Letting the client's experience touch yours. In *Changes*, **13**(4).

van Deurzen-Smith, E. (1988). *Existential Counselling in Practice*. London: Sage.

van Deurzen-Smith, E. (1989). What is existential analysis? In *Journal of the Society for Existential Analysis*, **1**.

van Deurzen-Smith, E. (1997). *Everyday Mysteries: Existential Dimensions of Psychotherapy*. London: Routledge.

van Deurzen-Smith, E. (1992). In Dryden, W. (ed.), *Hard-earned Lessons for Counselling in Action*. London: Sage.

van Deurzen-Smith, E. (1984). Existential therapy. In Dryden, W. (ed.), *Individual Therapy in Britain*. London: Harper and Row.

van Deurzen-Smith, E. (1990). Existential therapy. In Dryden, W. (ed.), *Individual Therapy: a Handbook*. Milton Keynes: Open University Press.

Viderman, S. (1988). 7 + 3 = (Seven plus three equals . . .). *Revue Française de Psychoanalyse*, **52**(3), 633–656.

Weldon, F. (1994). *The Curse of Therapy*. Times Dillon Debate.

Wilson, C. (1956). *The Outsider*. London: Victor Gollancz.

Winnicott, D.W. (1965). *The Family and Individual Development*. London: Tavistock.

Winnicott, D.W. (1958). *Collected Papers*. London: Tavistock.

Wittgenstein (1961). *Tractatus Logico-Philosophicus* (transl. Pears, D.F. and McGuiness, B.F.). London: Routledge and Kegan Paul.

Yalom, I. (1980). *Existential Psychotherapy*. New York: Basic Books.

Yeats, W. (1950). *Collected Poems of W.B. Yeats*. London: Macmillan.

Zimmerman, M.E. (1981). *Eclipse of the Self*. Athens, OH: Ohio University Press.

INDEX

Index compiled by Mary Kirkness

Related titles of interest...

Case Studies in Existential Psychotherapy and Counselling

Simon Du Plock

Provides a brief introduction to existential psychotherapy, and applies the concepts to a wide range of mental health problems through the life-cycle, including health and personal development processes.

0-471-96192-2   218pp   1997   Hardback
0-471-97079-4   218pp   1997   Paperback

Existential Time-Limited Therapy
The Wheel of Existence

Freddie Strasser and Alison Strasser

While there are various brief therapy models on the market, this book combines existential ideas into a structured time-limited modular approach. It represents an overview of the principal existential ideas and then applies them to the model, using case vignettes throughout.

0-471-96308-9   170pp   1997   Hardback
0-471-97571-0   170pp   1997   Paperback

Psychology in Counselling and Therapeutic Practice

Jill D. Wilkinson, Elizabeth A. Campbell, with contributions by Adrian Coyle and Alyson Davis

This book is a concise text and accessible reference book dealing with the areas of psychology which particularly support and enlighten the practice of counselling and psychotherapy. By bringing psychology into the consulting room, the authors ensure that psychological theory and research are accessible and applicable to the therapist's work with clients.

0-471-95562-0   286pp   1997   Paperback

Brief Rational Emotive Behaviour Therapy

Windy Dryden

Provides concepts in the context of a brief therapy process. Practitioners will find useful insights and guidance on applying these methods throughout the process of therapy, including building the working alliance, assessment, formulation, and work in sessions and outside the sessions. The whole process is illustrated by a case study which reflects the problems of real life work with a client.

0-471-95786-0   244pp   1995   Paperback

Visit the Wiley Home Page at http://www.wiley.co.uk